Molasses, Fatback, and Biscuits

*A story about a rural Carolina boy,
my father, Henian Edward Newsome*

by
Douglas Jay Newsome, Ed.D.

Molasses, Fatback, and Biscuits
by Douglas Jay Newsome, Ed.D.

All rights reserved
Copyright © 2017 by Douglas J. Newsome

ISBN: 978-0-692-89396-8

No part of this publication may be reproduced, stored in a retrieval system, or transmitted in any form or by any means electronic, mechanical, photocopying, recording, or otherwise, without the written permission of the author or publisher.

Table of Contents

Preface v
Early Life 1
Queen Bee – Laura 18
My Dad, My Friend 25
Big Brother – Andrew 34
No Power, No Electricity, but Oh the Eating Was Good 40
Fried Herrings 43
Salting and Smoking Meats 48
And Vegetables 52
The Hunt 54
Christmas Vittles 57
Adjusting to Army Meals 59
Beginning Primer Grades at Four 61
Just Country Life 82
Fishing with Grandma 86
My Passion – Baseball 89
A Radio 92
Our Pets 94
The Pleasure of Recreational Intoxicants 96
My Wife and Life-Long Love, Essie Nora 101
Drafted into the US Army 108
Basic Combat Training 112

- Advanced Individual Training 123
- March to War 129
- Our Officers 134
- My Second Tour of Duty 142
- Fort Monmouth 144
- Becoming A Radio Operator 148
- Fort Rucker — Alabama 156
- Nuclear Weapons 158
- New MOS Supply 161
- Civilian Life 170
- Retirement in Ahoskie 176
- The Church 179
- Politics 182
- Society and the Need for Change 192
- About the Author 197

Preface

My son tells me that I am a "Griot." He says that Griots have an historical tradition—particularly in West Africa, but I suppose throughout the world—of reciting oral history.

In West Africa, Griots were the primary means of passing along history from generation to generation, and thus pass along a society's culture, values, and norms. The roles of Griots are especially important in places where a majority of the population is illiterate.

The place where I grew up—an extremely small town called Winton in Hertford County, North Carolina—is not illiterate, but I don't believe that there is a lot written about my people. The West African Griots were traveling storytellers, poets, musicians, or they possessed a combination of these talents. I am not a musician or a poet, although I have memorized a few poems over the years. No, I am but a simple man, with one story to tell. The story that I have to tell is the story of my life, which I have been passing on orally all of my life. Now it is to be penned so people far and wide will know about the culture of Winton/Ahoskie, North Carolina.

I don't know about being a Griot, but I do think that I have a pretty good memory of the events of my past 92 years here on this earth, dating back to my early childhood. If I can make it another seven years, which I expect to do, I will have lived a century—100 years. Over this period, I have traveled the globe, and I have seen a lifetime of changes.

You see, I was born in a little house on the banks of the Chowan River on December 24, 1924. They say I was a Christmas gift to my parents. I was delivered at home by a midwife, and I imagine that my mother had no formal prenatal care. Few babies today in the twenty-first century are delivered outside of a hospital by untrained physicians, at least in civilized societies.

As a child, I survived a serious head injury where a neighbor hit me on the head with a hoe at about the age of three, and thereafter I suffered seizures until about the age of fourteen. I was never treated medically for this disorder. Instead, the female elders of the community treated me with a homemade remedy—they had me chew tobacco as a treatment.

The community in which I was reared had little to no technology. We had no automobiles, no running water, no electricity, no television, no telephones, certainly no cell phones, no computers, no Internet, no email, no texting, no Facebook, and no twittering. Sure, technology existed—Henry Ford had invented the Model T Ford decades earlier, and there were airplanes transporting people all over the world. I knew these amenities existed, as I read the newspaper and was exposed to some of them when I would visit uncles and aunts a world away (although that "world away" was only about 50 miles). Today, these items are not deemed luxuries but basic essentials for life.

My brother, mom, dad, and myself lived in a small, three-room house for most of my childhood. Despite the relatively small size of the house, it seemed as if we always had guests living with us—family or friends. At one point after my grandparents' house caught fire and burned down, we had nine people living in that house. We were but one big family socializing, eating, and praying together. Indeed, God was a powerful force in our lives, as God was in the lives of the people in our community.

I attended church and was taught to pray at an early age, and I continue to pray today. As a child, my favorite bedtime prayer was as follows: "Now I lay me down to sleep, if I die before I wake, pray the Lord my soul to take. Happy Jesus' sake. Amen."

My life's story is about building a life from just the basics and an extremely supportive extended family and network of friends, along with love, hard work, and determination. My parents were not overly educated, but they ensured that my brother and I graduated from high school and had the essentials for living life in the twentieth and twenty-first century.

When I talk about having the essentials for life, certainly we ate well, but the food we ate was the product of backbreaking work with our hands. We didn't have grocery stores, so we grew just about everything we consumed. We always had a garden and grew enough fresh fruit and vegetables to last us a year, with the proper canning techniques. Oh yeah, we also always, always had chickens. Farmers in the community also raised cattle, hogs, and sheep that we slaughtered, butchered, and preserved by smoking and salting. We never had an overabundance of food. We were living during the greatest depression this country had ever seen, but we had plenty to ensure that we didn't starve and were healthy.

I grew up with love and a nuclear and extended family—grandparents, parents, a brother, uncles, aunts, cousins, and friends. These were people who genuinely cared about my well-being. Early on, I spent a lot of time with my grandparents, as Mom and Dad worked. Although Granddad ran a farm, he didn't work it—his sons and grandsons worked the farm. Granddad oversaw their work, but he also had a lot of time on his hands. I was Granddad's constant companion. He was a good man who never cursed, but when irritated he had this saying: "The devil and Tom Walker." I can still hear him today.

My grandmother also allowed me to hang out with her in the kitchen or on the porch where she prepared meals and canned vegetables for the year. Most importantly for me, however, was that she took me with her on her favorite past-time, fishing. Sometimes, it would be just the two of us; at other times, it was a family gathering, with uncles, aunts, parents, and cousins.

I absolutely loved Granddad and Grandma, but my number one relationship was with my father. He was my best friend. Of course, I was very close with my older brother, but my favorite person in the world was my dad. I remember as a child that on many Saturdays, Dad and I would walk an 18-mile round trip to pick up his weekly pay. We'd walk the nine miles to get the money, then get some vittles at the local store and stop and visit with different family and friends on our return trip home. I always wanted to be around Dad. I was with him at his death and had to make the decision to have his leg amputated. The leg was amputated because of complications related to diabetes. Dad never recovered from the amputation, and I believe that resulted in his death.

Mom, on the other hand, was the Queen Bee of the family, making sure I learned the important lessons of life so that I could and would succeed. It was because of my mother's relationship with educators that I started school informally at the age of four, something unheard of back then. She made sure I had breakfast and lunch daily and clean, well-maintained clothing. Mom ensured that we did our chores on a daily basis, and chores back then were work—gathering firewood daily, bringing water to the house, feeding the chickens, collecting their eggs, and doing our homework.

And oh yeah, Mom beat my butt when I needed it. Well, in reality, I probably needed it more than she knew.

My best childhood friend was my cousin Ernest. He was my mischief-making partner. We were the same age and spent hours and hours together, either alone or with Granddad. I was with Ernest when he learned a very painful lesson about dealing with mules. I remember Ernest getting the air kicked out of him when he insisted that the mule do something the mule didn't want to do—work.

On another occasion, Ernest and I were thrown high in the sky from a cart being pulled by out-of-control mules. We survived with minor injuries. It's a wonder, though, that during our childhoods we didn't get seriously injured or killed. Country life was dangerous.

And then there was Essie Nora, my life-long partner, whom I also outlived. I had the privilege of nursing her through her final days here on this earth. Essie Nora suffered from Alzheimer's for approximately ten years before her death and had a steady decline. Even so, I wish she were here today. I always say I didn't find her, she found me. She was the glue that held the family together when I was away from home playing soldier. She ensured that our four children completed college and that three obtained terminal doctorate degrees. It was more Essie Nora than I who made sure the three boys grew up as responsible, spirit-filled men and that Sheila grew into womanhood. Essie Nora certainly found me, but I made sure that I didn't lose her.

This is the story of my life—as essay or manuscript about the culture of an African American farm boy who grew up in rural America during the Great Depression. The story of a boy who grew up eating molasses, fatback, and biscuits for breakfast and taking his lunch to school in an old, tattered pipe tobacco can inherited from his grandfather.

The story of Henian Edward Newsome is about a country boy who enlisted in the US Army, traveled the globe, and became the first African American atomic/nuclear bomb technician when most of the other African Americans were truck drivers, cooks, or orderlies. In my lifetime, I saw an Army with a commonly held belief by many whites, probably most, that African Americans were lazy, shiftless, untrustworthy, irresponsible, and unintelligent. Whites, educated or not, including the officer corps, did not trust black folk to supervise black folk. However, that Army and the United States changed over the years and saw that an African American, Colin Powell, was promoted to a four-star general, chairman of the Joint Chiefs of Staff; the highest-ranking and senior-most military officer in the United States Armed Forces. Additionally, as of this writing, the Army has Lt. General Nadja West, a three-star general; General West is the highest-ranking female ever to graduate from the US Military Academy at West Point; and the Navy currently has a four-star African American female admiral, Michelle Howard. The crown jewel was the election of Barak Obama as President of the United States of America, the "Commander in Chief."

Time heals but battle scars remain, and we have much further to go on race relations. Even so, I am proud to be an American.

I feel that my life was and is successful. I, like you, should be the one to determine what makes a successful life, but again my success didn't happen because my parents coddled me. They let me be a boy, but they had expectations. I worked hard around the house doing chores that only someone from the country who has no running water or electricity in the home could understand. And when the chores were done, I did homework by candlelight. I am successful because, as a boy, I had some responsibility for helping to put food on the table by hunting and gardening.

After 92 years, I may have confused some facts, confused some names, and misspelled others. I recognize that others may have viewed history differently; but I do feel as if this transcript represents, quite factually, my life. I don't know that I have a real legacy, but I do want my decedents, and the decedents of others who grew up during the Depression poor but happy, to know how I did it.

When we first started this process, my son asked me how I handled the highs and lows of my life. I stated that I didn't have real highs or real lows—I just played the hand I had been given. Today, I might say that my interactions with my family, nuclear and extended (wife, children, children-in-law, grandchildren, great-grandchildren, parents, brother, grandparents, uncles, aunts, cousins, teachers, both formal and informal, and friends), as well as my time in the Army, make up more of the pleasant memories. The death of my wife in particular and other close relative are more negative experiences, but all-in-all, I have lived a good life.

Some portions of this book might interest the reader more than others, and therefore I encourage the reader to utilize the table of contents. Start reading at a section that particularly interests you and skip around as you read. Read some, put it down for a day, week, or longer, and then come back and partake a bit more of rural North Carolina history, culture, and life. I was absolutely fortunate, but you will see that there were many others who grew up in the small community of Hertford County, North Carolina who had much greater success than I.

This story is not just about Hertford County but also this great country of ours, the United States of America, where there is opportunity. It requires work, determination, and some luck to achieve, but we are a nation of achievers. I happen to be an African American, and I do believe that we face many barriers to achievement, but as the old folk used to say, a black person had to work twice as hard to achieve, so we got to do what we got to do, work hard and achieve.

Again, this is not only my story but also the story of my family and friends, our African American culture, which I think should not be forgotten. This is the story about a boy who turned into a man, who was raised in a family where discipline was employed, but where there was also lots of love and an overriding faith in God.

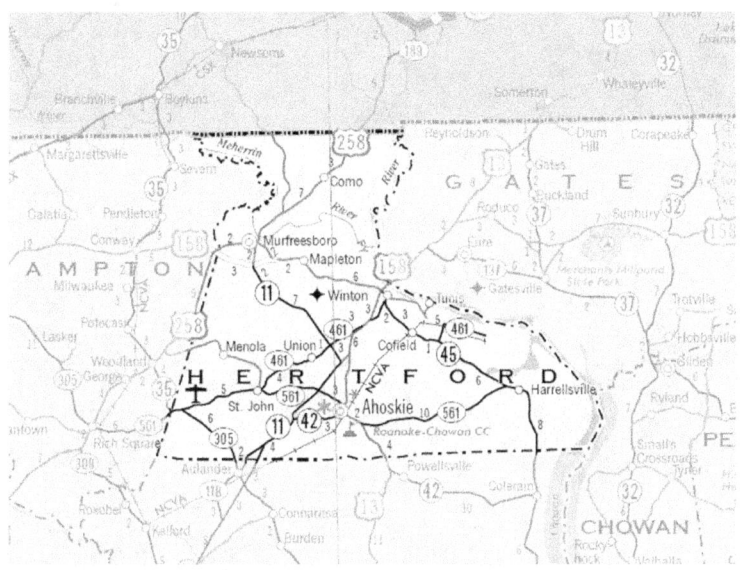

Hertford County, NC

Early Life

I was born to Henian and Laura Newsome on December 24, 1924, at about 5 p.m. in a tiny house on the bank of the Chowan River in Winton, North Carolina. No, I was not born in a hospital, and there were no doctors or nurses at my delivery; there was only my mother and a midwife. As a child/adolescent, on my birthday, I would sit looking at the clock waiting for 5 o'clock to come, my birth time.

Winton was and is the county seat for Hertford County, North Carolina. In 1924, its population was about 490, with a racial makeup of 68% African American; 28% Caucasian; and 2% Native American. Winton is one of Herford County's six towns, the others being Ahoskie, Como, Harrellsville, Murfreesboro, and St. John's.

In 1924, the population of the county was about 16,000. Today, it is approximately 24,000. The largest town in the county is Ahoskie. Ahoskie, being the largest city, serves as the hub for the county, and today I kind of view the other towns as suburbs of Ahoskie. Of course, the citizens of those towns probably view themselves as independent.

Ahoskie's racial makeup pretty much mirrors that of Winton's. Ahoskie's nickname is "The Only One" because no other town in the world is known by the same name. The origin of the word Ahoskie, which was originally spelled "Ahotsky," came from the Wyanoke Indians, a tribe native to the area.

My earliest memories date back to when I was about four years old, somewhere around 1928, about the time that I started school. I remember that my mother, dad, and I lived on my grandfather's, Reddick Newsome's, farm. Reddick was born in 1867, maybe two years after the Civil War ended, and he died in 1953, I think just a month before the birth of our second child, Marcus.

In 1928, not only was my grandfather a farmer but also my uncles were farmers, my cousins were farmers, and even my father was a farmer. All I can remember about my dad as a farmer is that they told me that he was a farmer because I can't remember him farming; on the other hand, I can remember vividly and in detail what my granddad did as a farmer: he supervised his sons, who did all of the work.

My dad would later inform me that farming was not the life for him. Farming was not to be his lifelong occupation not because the work was excessively hard—he did plenty of hard work—but because he realized that he couldn't support his family by farming. The white person who owned the farm, I believe that his name was Boone, made sure that the black sharecroppers could/would never break even financially and would always be in debt to him. Therefore, by default, he held the tenants in involuntary servitude. My dad was just not having it. On the other hand, farming was in my grandfather's blood. It was his way of life. It was his lifelong vocation, and it was the way he supported his family, to include his extended family.

I remember that when we lived on my grandfather's farm, we lived in a little house a couple of hundred yards from my grandfather's house, which by the way was a much larger house. His house needed to be larger because he had an army of relatives living with him.

Reddick Newsome lived with his wife, my grandmother, whom I also dearly loved, Mary Weaver. Three of his children also lived there—Martha, Jessie, and Reddick Jr. All were probably five to fifteen years my senior. They were older, but I never called them aunt or uncle. The rest of my granddad's and grandmother's children had moved out on their own or were deceased by then. They included Claudie, Genie, Mary, Ethel, Virginia, Lizzie, and Henian (my dad). Granddad also had a number of grandchildren living with him, my first cousins, Selma (maybe ten years older than me) and Jonnie (maybe four years older than me); both were Claudia's children—my oldest aunt on my father's side. She died in 1927, and I suspect that Selma and Jonnie had nowhere else to go but to their grandparents'. Claudia's older children were living on their own, and their oldest brother, Obadiah, was killed several years earlier. Selma never went to school to my knowledge, and I don't recall Jonnie going to school. I have no recollection why, although Jonnie certainly could have been in school. I do know that Selma and Jonnie didn't just lay around the house; they were also my granddad's farmhands.

I can remember many of my aunts, uncles and cousins visiting Granddad and Grandma, and after we moved off of their farm, I could barely wait to get back to their house any chance I could because there was always excitement and a house full of people. Some of my cousins were close to my age; others were older than some of my uncles and aunts.

When we were living on my granddad's property, in order to get to his house from ours, we had to go through a path with weeds and trees on both sides of the path. We then had to cross this big open field, or it seemed to be a big field to me at the age of four, where various crops were grown. The land was tilled during the spring, crops were grown in the summer, and harvested in the fall. This left the field barren during the winter.

Granddad's house seemed huge to me. It was one of those old, big, two-story houses. The main part of the house was two stories, but there was also a little part of the house towards the back that was only a single story. The house had a big porch, where we spent many summer evenings socializing. The porch had a roof that shielded us from the rain in the summer and the scorching sun. You had to go out of the main house and across the porch to get from one part of the house to the other. In inclement weather, we just accepted the fact that we might be a little uncomfortable getting from one part of the house to another.

This was routine living at the time, for if we had to go to the bathroom, even in the dead of winter and the blackest night, we had to leave the house entirely. We had no indoor plumbing or bathroom, so we would have to go to an outhouse (toilet) typically in the back yard, some distance from the house, to relieve ourselves.

My mom, dad, brother Bob, myself, and the numerous relatives/friends who boarded or lived with us on an almost constant basis all lived in the little house a couple of hundred feet from Granddad's. Our house was much, much smaller than Granddad's, as mentioned. Our house was about a two- or three-room house. The house was such that there were no specific bedrooms, but then again, all of the rooms were bedrooms.

Our kitchen had a little porch, and you had to go outside to get to the kitchen from the main section of the house, but the little porch didn't have a roof covering it. We had a little shelf out there on the porch where we always kept a wash pan and bucket of water. This wash pan and water was out there so that we could wash our hands and stuff like that as we had no running water. No running water, no indoor toilets, and no electricity was the norm for the time. These things were luxuries, and we could barely afford the necessities, let alone luxuries.

Both our house and Granddad's house were heated with wood stoves—one in the kitchen, and there may have been multiple wood stoves in the other part of the house primarily used for heating. However, many houses, including our small house, also had fireplaces. In our house, the wood stove in the kitchen also served as the cooking stove. And as you might expect, it could get really hot in spots in the house, particularly around the wood stove or fireplace in the winter time, given the heating source. But it also got pretty cold at times, especially at night when the fire went out. If we wanted to stay warm, we had to constantly feed those wood stoves/heaters/fireplaces, and this meant that we had to always have a supply of wood on hand. The wood was typically stored outside the house, a little portion on the porch, but most of it was across the yard in the woods to protect it from rain and such. Ensuring that there would be an ample supply of wood was backbreaking work. One had to cut down trees, chop the wood, and stack the wood so that it would be readily available for cooking and to heat the house on cold days and nights. Guaranteeing that there was a sufficient amount of wood for the winter was a year-round task, and it was the job of all of the boys or "menfolk."

Because the sun went down early in the wintertime, the family typically went to bed fairly early. When the sun went down, the house was only lit with an oil lamp. We used lamps with mirrors to magnify the light a little. When we retired to bed, we kept warm with layers and layers of quilts, which were made at quilting parties. A quilting party was an event where the women in the community would get together, talk, tell stories, and stitch together pieces of material into quilts. The women would alternate the homes where the parties were to be held.

We had mattresses on all of the beds in the house, but those mattresses were nothing like the ones we sleep on today. Back then, if one wanted real comfort, some of the ladies would maybe stitch together double mattresses filled with down (goose feathers). They called this a thicket, I believe, and it was composed of the soft feathers of the goose (down), not the outside feathers that help the goose keep the water out.

Our home was furnished with a couple of rocking chairs that were kept forever, and if the seats wore out, we would take it to somebody in the neighborhood who would repair it. Sugarcane reed was the basic material used to make seats for the chairs we used. In my neck of the woods, there was always an entrepreneur or someone who had special talents, and everyone knew where to find the right person for a particular problem or job. Typically, that person didn't have an office or a telephone, so communication was sent to him via word of mouth, traveling from person to person until it reached the desired party.

The Cotton School was just down the path from our house. Martha and Jessie would stop by our house, pick me up in the morning, and escort me to school. At the end of the day, they would drop me off before heading back home.

The Cotton School was just down the road from what we called California on the Big Mary Road (The Big Mary Road was where we lived for a time when I attended the Cotton School). They tell me that Big Mary ran a speakeasy back then, and everyone from miles around would visit. She was so popular that she had a road named after her.

The school was about six miles from Ahoskie, four or five miles from Winton, and maybe eight to ten miles from Murfreesboro. The area where I grew up was an extremely rural area, and once we moved off of my granddad's farm, there were no neighbors in the immediate vicinity. Visualize for a moment a small two- or three-room house in the middle of nowhere without any street lights (everyone in the country appreciated a full moon because we had natural light at night, the only time we had natural light) - that was rural North Carolina.

My granddad's house burned down some time before I turned 12 years old. After that, he, my grandma, uncles, aunts, and cousins came to live with us in our tiny house. No one was inconvenienced, as that was what we did for family back then.

Our home was an open home for family and friends and we almost always had someone visiting or living with us. When granddad's house burned down, that was the most people we had living with us at any one time, about nine people.

The first person that I can remember who came to live with us was Jonah Vann. Jonah was Claudia's stepson by her second husband, who came to live with us for about a year around the time of his mother's death. Jonah was my father's nephew and my first cousin, and he was older than my uncles and aunts still living with my grandparents.

When Jonah lived with us, he earned his keep, as he worked right alongside my dad on Dad's portion of the farm. After my dad stopped farming, Jonah just kinda drifted away. He just disappeared, as his services were no longer needed. I think that he probably made his way to Suffolk, Virginia, which was approximately 30 miles from Pleasant Plains where his dad, Thomas, had settled.

Jonah and I never had any deep conversations. After all, Jonah was maybe 19 years old, and I was only four, but I really liked Jonah. I know that Selma, one of Jonah's half-brothers, remained in the area, and forty years after Jonah moved away in the 1970s, I remember Selma traveling to Suffolk, Virginia to visit Jonah and his half-sisters. My last contact with Jonah was in the late 1960s or early 1970s, after I retired from the

US Army. I was living on Snipes Street, in Ahoskie, North Carolina, and commuting to my job at the Norfolk Naval Base in Norfolk, Virginia. My car broke down, and while the car was being repaired, I roomed with none other than Jonah. This time, I lived with Jonah at his pad in Suffolk. We had come full circle.

Suffolk is about halfway between Ahoskie and Norfolk, and there were commuter buses transporting employees to the Naval Base from Suffolk. As I think back, Jonah was just a good, down-home, homeboy. He was never a drinker, just a hard worker. First, with my dad, and later, I know he worked in the peanut factories in Suffolk, Virginia. Suffolk was/is often identified as the peanut capital of the world.

After that lone year that my father farmed, our family moved off my grandfather's farm onto the main road, where the Cotton School was located. We lived there maybe one year, then relocated to Little California a couple of miles away.

About three years after we moved from my grandparent's farm, I guess I was in the neighborhood of six or seven years old, one of my granddad's daughters, Lizzie, was having problems with her husband, Tom Doughty. My granddaddy wasn't having any of that nonsense, so he sent his sons out to fetch Lizzie, and subsequently Lizzie and her two children came to live with my granddaddy in the big house. I was delighted when Aunt Lizzie and her two children came to live with Granddad because that meant I had two additional playmates.

Her youngest son was Ernest, who was just about my age. I was three months older than Ernest, who was born in March of 1925; whereas, I was born in December of 1924.

Ernest and I would become the best of pals. We frequently tagged along with my granddad as he moved about the farm.

Annie, who was about seven years older than I was, and Ernest, were always close. After I retired from the Army and Postal Services, and returned to my roots in the Ahoskie, Annie and I would visit frequently, as we lived less than two blocks from each other.

As mentioned, we only had the essentials for life living in rural North Carolina, and that meant that our only means of transportation, at least for my immediate family, was to walk, catch a bus, or hope that someone would extend a ride to us if we needed to travel significant distances. Also, bicycling was one of our most dependable forms of transportation. We never had a horse and buggy, so when we needed to go somewhere, we frequently "rode the road on foot."

My granddad, on the other hand, had mules and a cart. I don't remember him having a buggy, but he might have had one at some time. The difference between a buggy and a cart is that a buggy was one of those luxury items, like the "Sunday Mobil." It was like a carriage that usually had only one cushioned bench seat. It was a two, maybe three-passenger vehicle at the most. Behind the bench seat there was a little area where a small person could sit down or where you might store some supplies.

The cart was the working man's truck. It was like a big wagon that had sides to it, so one could seat a lot of people in it, or materials for farming. I remember riding with my granddaddy in the cart, as he would take me with him different places, such as when he would go to Ahoskie to get his cornmeal. I first started riding with him at about the age of four, and when Ernest came a couple of years later, Granddad would take the two of us out with him.

About the horse and cart, well, really it was a mule and cart, and the mule was a multiple purpose animal, used as much for pulling the plow as it was for pulling the cart. When it came time for replacing a mule, Granddad would contact Boone. Boone would drop by Granddad's farm with some old cripple mules for viewing and sell him one or two mules for maybe $25.00 each.

My granddad was a tenant sharecropper, and he rented a portion of the Boone's farm. My grandparents disliked Boone, especially Grandma, who used to call him Big Belly Boone. Granddad was a farmer supervisor, supervising his boys and grandboys, who did all of the work on the farm. He had three mules, and he would have the boys or grandboys, often as young as 13, do all of the plowing. Those boys and mules worked hard, tilling that piece of land and tending to the livestock for little gain. My granddad would never even hitch the mules to the cart, even if he wanted to run an errand or travel somewhere like to Ahoskie. No, when it came time for him to go somewhere, he would tell one of the boys to go hitch the mule to the cart and get it ready so that he could make a trip. The boys would be dutiful and do as they were told. They would hitch the mule to the cart and bring it around to the front of the house, and as most occasions would have it, I would be off for a ride.

One day after a trip when me, Granddaddy, and Ernest had gotten back to the house, Granddad gave the mule and cart to one of the boys to put up. He told his son to make sure that the old mule got something to drink before he put him in the barn because he knew that the old mule was thirsty. Granddaddy then went into the house, leaving me and Ernest to engage in our usual mischief. While the mule was drinking, Ernest and I jumped up in the cart. My uncle had neglected to tie the old mule up, and after the mule got all the water he wanted, he decided to take off on a run. Not a leisurely trot but a run.

There were a number of trees in the yard that had big roots jutting out above the ground, so when the old mule took off running, the cart hit one of those roots and threw the cart off the wheels. One of the wheels went over the fence. The yard was fenced in because Granddad was a farmer, and he needed to keep the livestock in the yard. Well, when the wheel came off of the cart, the cart flipped me and Ernest off, and we went flying, eventually landing hard on the ground. Fortunately, neither of us got hurt, although we thought we were hurt. Of course, Granddad and Aunt Lizzie came running out of the house to rescue us, petting us up initially before scolding us.

Another incident that occurred where Ernest was injured had to do with the two of us working together. On this particular day, Ernest was driving the mule and cart from the field where we had to collect the tobacco. It was our job to fill the cart with the tobacco that had been pulled by the primers and bring it back to the tobacco barn. On this day, that old stubborn mule got halfway back to the barn and wouldn't go any further, and Ernest was impatient. Mules are stubborn creatures, so Ernest started hitting and whipping the mule with the control lines, but this mule was not going anywhere. Well, Ernest got off the cart and moved closer to the mule in order to whip him harder, and that old mule kicked him in the stomach. Ernest let out the biggest scream I had ever heard, and of course I broke down laughing. Ernest had learned his lesson and waited patiently until that old mule was ready to move on. From that point on, Ernest always worked at the mule's pace. Certainly, my wife understood mule behavior and would often use it to describe me. She would say, "You're as stubborn as a mule."

On Granddad's farm, there were a whole bunch of livestock. Although when I say a whole bunch, I don't really know how many. To me, as a young child, four, five, or six would have been a whole bunch. There were cows, a bunch of hogs, a whole bunch of chickens, guinea fowl, and a bunch of sheep. In order to manage all of these animals, the farm had to be large so that there was sufficient land for the animals to graze.

All of the animals were raised for slaughter except the cows, which were primarily kept for milking. The sheep had a dual purpose: they were raised for their wool as well as to be slaughtered and sold or bartered for work, food, or other items. I remember each year during the spring when it began to get warm, this guy would come around with sheers and clippers and cut the wool off all of the sheep. I don't know what the person who clipped the sheep's wool did the remainder of the year, but he was extremely proficient at his trade and would sheer each sheep of its wool in a couple of minutes.

The chickens were good for slaughter or killing any time, and on any given Sunday, we would have a chicken for dinner. That same chicken was walking the yard the previous day or two. The hens were the last to go because of their value in producing eggs. Eggs were a staple food supply for the family. We always had eggs, and I don't know what I would have done for lunch had it not been for the fried eggs I would take to school on almost a daily basic.

But as I mentioned, sharecroppers had a hard time winning. The guy that owned and rented the farm to my granddad would come around the house at least once or twice a week, and he would collect his share of eggs and anything else that he wanted. I say wanted because he was getting filthy rich off those poor sharecroppers, including my granddad, but he continued to come over and leach. Granddaddy also had a grapevine that produced these big scuppernong grapes, and you could bet come harvesting time the owner of the property would come by and collect grapes and fruit from our fruit trees and all kinds of goodies. I don't know of the owner collecting pigs or sheep or milk, but I imagine that he probably did because he got whatever he wanted. Of course, back then, many of the sharecroppers were African American, and the landowners were always white, so there was always animosity between the two. Although the sharecroppers may have been polite in the presence of the owner, they generally hated him.

My dad saw that this arrangement was not a healthy one, and he made sure he didn't get trapped. He severed his arrangement with the landowner after only one year of renting from him.

In 1929, the year my granddad stopped farming, we had to move off the farm, but we didn't move far from Granddad—maybe a mile at most—and that allowed us to visit often. Even after the move, I was Granddad's regular companion, frequently tagging along with him. I was sure that I was the favorite, as Granddad would take me everywhere with him. Ernest also went along a lot and probably thought he was the favorite.

I remember going out with my granddad one day, way out to the back of the pasture to the farthest piece of land on the farm where the boys were working. The farm was divided by a creek behind the house, and one had to cross that creek and travel a considerable distance to get to the back of the farm. On this particular day, I noticed that my granddad was continuously looking up at the sky, more than usual, so as he looked up, I looked up. After a while, I saw a dark cloud come up. The boys didn't seem to notice the cloud, as they continued to plow the land. My granddad knew what the cloud meant. He realized that a storm was coming our way, so he had the boys unhitch the mules from the plows and hitch them to the cart; he had decided that it was time to go in. By the time we got all hitched up to go and began heading home, it started raining, and it was coming down hard. Along with the rain, it too started to hail. Granddad had those mules flying down that path and his hat flew off. The hail started beating him on the head, and he was hunched over me, covering me up – protecting me, and he had a phrase that he would use when he got angry or frustrated. I never heard him use a curse word. Instead of cursing when he got angry or frustrated, he would say, "The Devil and Tom Walker." He used that phrase repeatedly on this particular day, as the hail beat him on the head after his hat flew off. He loved that hat and always wore it, but that day it was lost because he didn't stop to go after it.

The events of the day got even worse because we had to stop and open one of the gates as we approached the house. We always kept the gate closed to keep the animals from getting either in or out. Well, we eventually made it home, and although it may not have been a pleasant experience for Granddad, to this day it is a fond memory for me because he demonstrated his love for me on that day more strongly than I could have ever imagined.

MOLASSES, FATBACK, AND BISCUITS

Me Just Chillin

Queen Bee - Laura

Laura Newsome, my mom, was as hard a worker as any woman in the 1920s, '30s, and '40s. She was not just a stay-at-home mother, but I can't imagine too many African American women at the time not working. Times were hard back then. During peanut season, Mom stacked peanuts, which was a very dirty and laborious job. Peanuts are roots, and someone has to dig the peanuts out of the ground. After the peanuts were dug up, someone had to pick the peanuts off the ground, shake them, and stack them on these long poles—maybe six feet or so—for drying.

During cotton season, Mom picked cotton. I've heard it said that African American women could and would pick up to 200 pounds of cotton daily. I don't know if Mom did, but if others did, I am certain that she did also.

In the dog days of summer, starting around July or August, she worked in the tobacco fields. Her job was looping tobacco or connecting/tying the leaves of the tobacco plant after they had been picked. She tied the leaves into bundles of maybe five to ten leaves so that each bundle could be placed on sticks, maybe an inch by one inch and six feet long. The sticks would then be hung in the tobacco barn for curing.

Mom also did laundry for the white folk. She would pick up their clothes, or they would drop them off at our place, and she would wash them, dry them, and then iron them. This was all completed with hard labor because there was no automation at the time. She washed the clothes by hand on a wash board in a big tub, hung the clothes out on the line to be dried by the wind and sun, and since there was no electricity, she used a flat iron heated from the wood stove to make it hot enough to iron wrinkles out of clothing. This meant that in the summertime, with the heat often hovering around 100 degrees in sweltering humidity, the wood stove would be burning. And boy could mom iron. I was voted the best dressed boy in school because of mom's ability to make my clothes standout. No, we didn't send many things to the cleaners, I don't know if they even had cleaners at the time; for us and those white folk, my mother was our cleaners.

As a child/adolescent growing up, I didn't really think about us being any better or worse off than any of the other families in the neighborhood. In my mind, we were just an average family. Thinking back on it, I think that we did have it better than most of my peers, as I really didn't have to work, nor did I have to farm like many of my peers had to. For sure there were only seven males in my fifty-person graduation class, and no the population in Hertfort County was not a seven-to-one female-to-male ratio. Certainly, I had plenty of male friends who didn't attend school. Many others didn't go to school regularly because they had to work primarily on the farm, so they continued to fail and eventually just stopped going. Even many of my male cousins never attended school.

My family had a steady source of income, as both Mom and Dad worked. In addition to that, my mother's brother, Rossi, had been killed in World War I, and my mother got his survivor's benefits of $28.00 monthly, so maybe we were a little better off financially than many other families in the neighborhood. I never knew why Uncle Rossi left his survivor's benefits to my mother as opposed to his other siblings. Maybe it was because she was somewhat sickly all her life, as I know that she suffered from chronic bronchitis. Back at that time, I never thought that we were better or worse off than other families in the neighborhood, but now that I think about it, T. S. Britt's family not only owned a radio but they also owned a car—so yes, I suppose there were families more financially stable than we were but again there were many, many worst off.

As mentioned, I was probably the exception when it came to working when I was an adolescent because I didn't. I tried selling newspapers for a while but didn't do too well. I had no transportation and had to walk long distances from house to house. The houses were just too far apart.

Although I didn't work outside of the home, I certainly did chores which were supervised by Laura Newsome. Life as a child growing up in rural North Carolina was not just leisure and games; we had to work, although the work we did around the house is much more than I expect children do today. I didn't really consider it work. It was something to do, and it kept me and Bob occupied. Bob and I were expected to hunt, which we did, and we contributed this to the supply of food for the family. It was work, but to us it was also a recreational activity and fun.

Since we had no electricity, we heated the house with wood in the wintertime, and Mom cooked year-round on a wood stove as well as using it for her laundry business. My dad would cut down the trees—with a one- or two-man saw when he wasn't working. Bob and I were required to use a cross cut saw to saw the tree trunk into about 12-inch lengths, with an ax chop the foot lengths pieces of wood so that it would fit into a stove and then stack the wood. This was work and not a recreational activity. Most of the wood was stacked in the woods, so daily we had to retrieve the wood and stack some on the porch. Some of the wood that we used in the stove or the fireplace was green wood, which would not readily burn, so we also had to gather lighter wood to make the pine burn better. Lighter wood is wood that we gathered from the trunks of trees that had previously fallen and was in a state of decay. These trunks don't automatically rot, but they become hard and brittle and occasionally flexible, and we called this kindling. Kindling burns like Kerosene, and this would immediately ignite the green wood.

Collecting wood was a daily activity. Mom may have had to remind us occasionally, but Bob and I were responsible, and completing our chores was something that we generally did automatically.

Mom also ensured that Bob and I did our homework, which really was not very onerous because Bob and I both liked school. During the school year, Bob and I had homework almost every night, and typically we had to get it done before dark because we had no electricity, so after dark, we either lit the house via candle or Kerosene Lamp. This lighting was not the best for doing homework. We had a couple of lamps with globes on them, to prevent them from blowing out, but we never had the fancy lamps with mirrors to project or amplify the light. In the wintertime, from the time we got out of school until bedtime, we were occupied with something to do and mom was our general manager who ensured that we completed our task.

Laura Newsome was also my disciplinarian. My mama beat my butt when she thought that I needed it, but on the other hand, Dad never even raised his voice towards me. I can never remember being angry at my father, ever—that is something to say. Dad and me, we got along brilliantly, but my relationship with my mama was different. It seemed that we just didn't get along. As a matter of fact, just a couple of days before she died, we got into an argument. Mama and I were like oil and water; we were always at odds, from the beginning or as early as I can remember until the end. Even so, she loved me and only wanted the best for me. I guess like Essie Nora said, I was just as stubborn as a mule. I know that Mama sacrificed for me big time, and I really appreciated all the things that she did for me.

The primary reason that I got spankings was the fights that I started with my brother Bob. In fact, the last time she spanked me was for getting into a fight with Bob. During this last spanking, she would spank me some, and I went right back to fighting him some more, and then she would spank me some more, and I went right back to fighting him again. Mom had to take breaks when spanking me because of her Bronchitis, she needed breaks to catch her breath and I was just not responding in the manner she wanted. The last time while she was spanking me, I just stood on the porch looking up at the sky, and she just gave up. I stopped fighting him, and that was the last time we got into a fight.

Mama really didn't need to spank me because Bob was older and larger and could beat me if he wanted. I guess that he was so beholden to the family for being taken in that he would never do anything to disrespect the family—or, on the other hand, he was just a very decent human being.

Momma

My Dad, My Friend

My dad Henian was frequently called Henan, I guess because a lot of people couldn't pronounce his given name. He was born on August 23, 1904 and died in 1969. He attended school to the seventh grade and, without a doubt, this was a significant achievement. At that time, very few African American males even attended school. A few of his brothers did not view school as something favorable and thus failed to attend on a regular basis or graduate. I guess Dad communicated to me that school was important, and he supported my education. Likewise, I would value education and communicate that to my children. All are college graduates, and three have doctorate degrees.

The first job I remember Dad having was as a farmer, but I can't tell you what he did as a farmer because I never saw him work as a farmer. I do remember Granddad and my uncles farming, but I can't remember Dad as a farmer. Maybe it is because Dad only farmed for one year—the year that I started school. Granddad, on the other hand, was a real farmer and farmed his entire life.

Just as education was valuable to my dad, so- too, was work—maybe not farming, but he was a worker. He spent much of his adult life engaged in hard, backbreaking work, much of it in the logging industry. He was a logger, which simply means that he went into the woods, often deep into the woods and swamps, with a team of men and cut down trees. Dad used a saw—either a single person or double (cross cut) person saw—and spent the day engaged in the backbreaking working of cutting down trees. Once the tree was "felled," they cut the branches off the trees.

Once the trees were cut down and the branches cut off, the trees would be loaded onto a truck and hauled down to the river. A truckload of logs was called a cord, and the team, including Dad, got paid by the cord. I don't know how much he earned, but I know it was not enough for the backbreaking work that he and the other loggers did.

The work was done in the swamp, and tractors, trucks, or even horses would have to go into the woods to pull the trees out so that they could be loaded on to trucks for transport. Loggers used what was called a "sketter" machine, which is an engine with a cable and a hook on the end. The hooks were connected to the logs, and the felled trees were pulled from the woods by horses, mules, tractors, trucks, or humans.

Before Dad transitioned out of the woods as a logger, he worked for a spell on the river front where the logs were transported after being brought out of the woods, but I am not sure exactly what he did on the river front. From the river front he went to work in the sawmill, where he cut the bark off the logs and shaved the planks into two-by-fours or two-by-eights, etc. He operated two saws, one stationary and the other mobile, so that he could adjust the width of the planks as he sawed. The thickness, width, and length of the planks could all be adjusted.

The logging industry was very dangerous, and many of the workers were killed or injured. Dad was seriously injured, and this eventually caused him to discontinue this line of work. Dad bruised and cut his lower leg/upper ankle while working in the woods, and the protective equipment that he wore caused the bruise to become infected. The protective equipment were these big boots that the men wore into the swamp to keep them as dry as possible. Of course, the work was hard and labor intensive, so they sweated, and by the end of many days, they were drenched anyway.

The sore just got worse; it wouldn't heal. I remember that there were times when his leg and ankle were maybe two or three times their natural size. He couldn't stop working though, because if he didn't work, he didn't get paid, and if he didn't get paid, the family couldn't survive. Back at that time, African Americans rarely went to the doctor, so the injury became chronically infected.

My brother Bob eventually found a doctor in Norfolk, Virginia, maybe 70 miles away, whose treatment was to strip the meat off the bone and replace it with grafted skin from his stomach, hip, and thigh. The leg then began to heal some, but he never regained full use of the limb and walked with a permanent limp thereafter.

Not being able to work in the log wood or sawmill industry because of an inability to walk or stand for long periods of time forced Dad into a different line of work. There was no such thing as Social Security disability, so he relied on the help of people in the community to get started in a new occupation. He became a small business owner. There was this vacant store on Highway 13, which was the route that the log trucks typically traveled to transport the logs to the river. Dr. Weaver's brother Lionia, who also owned a number of logging trucks, owned this store. I am not sure why the store was empty, but my dad approached Lionia about opening the store and was told to go ahead and open it. He said they would talk about the amount of rent he would pay later, after he made a little money. This was a world where people helped people for the sake of doing the right thing.

In the beginning, the store was stocked with sodas, soda crackers, sardines, Vienna sausage, pottage meat, and other such things. Dad made that store work, probably because it was in a prime location, and he was a very social, friendly, and likable person. He was one of them, a logger, and knew many of the truck drivers and crews working in the logging industry. It is certainly good to be friendly and have friends.

With time, Dad was able to stock and sell candy, cookies, cheese, canned goods, meats, handkerchiefs, pocketknives, and other essentials, like tobacco products (yes, tobacco products were essential back then—everyone used some form of tobacco; cigarettes, snuff, or chewing tobacco). His general store attracted a wide range of customers, but most were poor or working class African Americans; however, the store was located directly across the street from C. S. Brown High School, so he got a lot of business from students, teachers, and school administrators as well.

Dad also allowed people to make purchases on credit. No, they didn't have a credit card; they would simply come into the store, select some items, and ask Dad to put their bill on the books. This just meant that Dad would log the purchase in a book, and when the client had money, they would stop by the store and make a payment. This was pretty routine for transactions at the time.

Working in the logging industry and running that store were Dad's primary occupations, but he also had a side job. Through much of his life, he was also an agent for a tailor company. He had this job as far back as I can remember, back to about the early 1930s. As a tailor, he had this little kit that fit into a small suitcase; in the case, there were different types of cloth samples and measuring tools. People would come by the house or the store if they needed or wanted a suit of clothes or some pants or something. Dad would measure them, they would select the fabric they wanted, and Dad would take their deposit and place the order for them. The company would then mail the finished product to the customer cash on delivery (COD).

Dad made sure that he ordered clothes for me and Bob through the company a couple of times a year. He would measure Bob and me and order us pants and suits as dressing nicely was important to both of us and our parents. Bob was older and always seemed to have a job, so he could also buy clothes. After he graduated, he continued to by nice threads (clothes). When Bob went into the military, I inherited his clothes. This, in addition to the clothes Dad ordered for me, contributed to my being selected as the best-dressed male in my senior class. Clothes are not the only thing that contributes to being well dressed, shoes are also important and I made sure that my shoes were always shined so well that you could see your image in them.

By the way, a good friend of mine, Lola Jones, was the best-dressed female. Lola was an excellent seamstress and made her own clothes, and I believe she eventually moved to Raleigh where she went into the clothing industry. Lola and I never dated, but we sat together in class. I suppose she sat close to me not because I was such a snazzy dresser but because I was good in math and was more than willing to help her out.

Like most parents, Dad was more concerned about me and Bob looking nice than himself. He was always clean, but I don't remember him wearing new clothes too often—Sunday being the day where he dressed his best.

Dad worked and got to work any way he could when he was working in the woods. Of course, there were weather conditions that didn't allow my dad and the crew to go into the woods, but they were few and far between. On most days they worked, and this meant that during the winter he was out of the house before daylight and didn't get back home until after dark. This made for a long day, and there was little time for recreational activities. It was off to work, back home, dinner, bed, and back to work. Oh, and he had no transportation other than Pat and Charlie (walking), or his bicycle, or bumming a ride from someone. So, this meant that in the dark, he would ride that bicycle the five or ten miles to the worksite or the pick-up point. Later, after he got the store, he walked the mile or so to the store seven days a week on that bad leg.

MOLASSES, FATBACK, AND BISCUITS

I loved my dad. We were extremely close when I was a child and best friends when I became an adult. I don't recall him every saying an ill word to me, and as a child, I always wanted to be around him. I can remember back when I was a child how I walked with Dad on Saturdays to go pick up his check. You see, back when I was growing up, people didn't have automatic deposit for their wages, nor did they get paid with a check. They got paid in cash. The boss didn't bring the money to you, and for my dad, the boss didn't pay him on workdays so he had to go get his earned money.

So every Saturday, Dad would have to walk to Tunis to get paid, and on many Saturdays, I walked along with him. The eighteen miles round trip was an all day task, and we made it as pleasant as possible. Early on Saturday morning, we would depart the house with an empty burlap sack and walk to Tunis—maybe three hours or so. I remember a place in Tunis, this little store where after Dad got paid, we would stop for food. The store allowed patrons to purchase things on credit, IOU, and if Dad had a bill, he would "pay what he had on the books." Dad then would purchase a few groceries: bread, bologna, cheese, maybe some soda crackers, and a soda pop or two. The bologna came in a loaf, and it would be cut to the length Dad wanted in multiple slices. We would eat lunch from what we had purchased, and what we didn't eat, we would put in the burlap sack and head back home.

On the way back home, we took a lot of breaks. We knew people along the way, and we would stop and chat for a while, then move on to our next family or friend's house, chat some more, and then move on. I tagged along on a regular basis.

Bob would go occasionally, but I always wanted to go. I didn't get to go as much as I wanted to because I had chores to do.

As a teenager, listening to boxing was one of our primary sources of entertainment. Somehow, Dad and I developed a tradition of shadow boxing as a form of greeting. This was a habit we engaged in until his death. Dad died in the hospital from complications related to diabetes. His injured leg got infected, and it had to be amputated. I was the one who signed the papers for the surgery. Unfortunately, he never recovered.

I feel bad about that decision today, but it was the only choice we had. We didn't know as much about diabetes back then as we do now, but we did know that someone with diabetes should watch their diet. My dad never watched his diet. He ate fried foods and loved, absolutely loved, my mother's biscuits and a bowl of peaches. This diet resulted in him being somewhat overweight to the point where his grandchildren called him big-daddy.

All in all, Dad was my role model. I can only wish that I was as much a role model to my children and others who I have come in contact with as Dad was to me.

*Dad – His grandchildren called him
Big Daddy – note his stomach*

Big Brother - Andrew

Bob and I married women from similar backgrounds. His wife Amaza's parents, Maner and James Parker, had 14 children, where Essie Nora's parents had 15 children. Essie Nora has two siblings still living at this writing, and Amaza is one of two children from her family still living. Both Essie Nora and Amaza were from the St. John areas of North Carolina, and both of their families were sharecroppers much of their lives. It is prophetic that Amaza and Bob adopted their oldest child, and Bob was adopted the oldest child into our family.

It is my understanding that Amaza's parents and my wife's parents were good friends most of their adult lives. Finally, Amaza and Essie Nora attended the same school, Robert L. Vann in Ahoskie.

Andrew (Bob) White came to live with us when I was probably five years old. Although his parents' last name was Whitehead, we always called him White. I don't know why, but we did, and I called him Bob, but my mom called him Andrew. He was informally adopted by my parents, as I am sure they never went through the legal process of a formal adoption.

Bob was born in 1921 sometime during the month of September. The exact date is unknown. I believe that he came to live with us in 1929 because I don't remember him walking to school with me, Martha, and Jessie that first year. Bob came to live with us because his mother, Rosa Bryan Whitehead, my mother's sister, died. I guess his father, Willie Whitehead, just wasn't in a position to take care of him. Bob still maintained a positive relationship with his father Willie, and I believe he visited him until Willie's death.

Although my parents never formally adopted Bob, he is the only sibling I ever had, and formal or not, he was the son of Henian Senior and Laura and my brother. My mother really rescued him, and I am grateful.

I always looked up to Bob, although I got into a lot of trouble because of him and maybe my jealousy of him, but I have always thought that he was more intelligent—although maybe he was just more mature or more appreciative of what he had because of his life prior to coming to live with us. Bob was also more athletic. He played school sports, baseball, when we were at the Pleasant Plains school, and he was a pretty good catcher. Bob got injured one day when he was playing a school from Ahoskie. He was injured by Julius Watford, Howard Hunters' (of Hunters Funeral Home in Ahoskie) wife's brother. Watford was at bat and hit a pop-up ball between the catcher's and pitcher's mound; the pitcher and catcher were both looking up and heading for the ball, and they collided and both wound up bleeding—the pitcher from the forehead, and Bob got a pretty big gash on his nose.

Bob would marry Amaza a year or two after he got out of the Army and they would have two children were named Andrew and Katrina. Bob met Amaza when he was a junior or senior in high school at Calvin S. Brown, and she was a student at Robert L. Vann in Ahoskie. They met at the Casaymia, a local dance hall, what Amaza calls a playground, located on Highway 13 maybe three miles from Ahoskie where almost all teenagers hung out. I was too young to get into the Casaymia at the time, so it was a while before I met her.

Bob was much more mobile than I was because he had friends whose parents had a car. His friends were the Mitchells who lived on Big Mary Road. There were three boys, and one was Bob's age but they were all close friends with Bob. One of the Mitchell boys was dating Amaza's sister, and he introduced Bob to Amaza; they began dating and eventually got married. I don't know what attracted Amaza to Bob, but it could have been his dress—he was a sharp dresser. He was the best dresser I knew, and as indicated before, he always had some odd job, so he had money to buy clothes with.

Anyway, Bob had a couple of pairs of trousers and suits. The suits he wore were Zoot Suits, known for long jackets and baggy pants that narrowed at the ankle. He also wore hats, nice hats, although nearly everyone wore a hat back in those days. Although Bob was a very good dresser, he was also very nice, calm, and levelheaded, and I imagine that he would have been a good catch for anyone, but Amaza was the lucky one.

Bob worked at the Norfolk Naval Base for forty years as a tool room attendant, until his death. He was also readily identified by the African American residents of the Berkley section of Norfolk, as he was a barber cutting hair at David Barber Shop in Norfolk, Virginia. I imagine for forty years also.

Dad and I were the closest, but Bob and I bonded and I certainly loved him and miss him as I miss everyone who has gone before me. I wish I hadn't been so jealous of him as a child and appreciated him more.

Andrew/Bob – My sharp dressing brother

Me, Momma, and Bob

Dad, Momma, Bob, Amaza, Essie Nora, Edward, Marcus, Douglas, Sheila, and the Dog

No Power, No Electricity, but Oh the Eating Was Good

When I was a child, most people in my neighborhood ate what they raised or engaged in some type of bartering with neighbors for meats (pork and beef); almost everyone had a garden, guns for hunting, fishing poles, and most people had chickens. People hunted for game, such as deer, rabbit, squirrel, opossum, and raccoon. Because not too many people had cattle or pigs, these were the things that people bartered for or brought.

In my home for breakfast, we would typically have molasses, fatback, and biscuits. This was a staple for African Americans living in rural North Carolina. Molasses was plentiful, as was the flour required for baking biscuits. You see, in the 1920s and '30s, one of the major crops of the area was sugarcane, a key ingredient for molasses. The way molasses was made was to first harvest the sugarcane, locally grown. The cane grows 8 to 10 feet, and after it is harvested, the cane would then be stripped down to a stalk. The stalk would then be loaded onto a cart and typically transported somewhere in the neighborhood or into town where there was a sugarcane press.

The press that I am used to seeing had an auger in the center, like a screw device connected to a long pole. The other end of the pole was connected or hitched to a mule. The mule would be encouraged to walk in a circle, making the auger grind and squeeze the juice or syrup from the cane stalks. The syrup was caught in a large pan, or what they used to call a vat, and the syrup would then be cooked. Not anyone could cook the syrup; there had to be an expert cooking it, typically a local expert. The cane couldn't be cooked too much, or it would become too thick, especially in the wintertime, when it got cold. On the other hand, one didn't want the molasses too thin either. Despite their proficiency, the cooks still screwed it up from time to time; anyone can have a bad day.

Making molasses was a tedious process, since it was cooked in a vat over open flame, not on a stove. If the cane was not cooked quite right, or it was kept too long, it would likely turn into sugar. Sugar was not the desired end product, molasses was.

In the wintertime, even good molasses would get thick, so when we heated it up for breakfast, most of the time we would pair the molasses with cooked fatback and fatback grease for a salty sweet taste. We would then get some biscuits and sop up this nectar. On the occasion when we didn't have molasses, we would just sop the grease from the fatback. This would be a typical breakfast for my immediate family and my grandparents, so I just assume that it was typical for the community in which I lived. People say that fatback is unhealthy, but my contemporaries lived to be in their 90s and even to 100 years old eating this breakfast.

Cornmeal was also a food staple upon which we relied in the 1930s and '40s. At the end of the harvest season, farmers had lots and lots of corn that was used for a variety of purposes. Some of the corn would be taken to the local mill to be ground into cornmeal. There was a mill about five miles or so from our house in Little California, which my granddad used for grinding the cornmeal. I would frequently ride with my granddad on trips where he transported his raw corn to be made into cornmeal. I never saw Granddad use money to have his corn ground into cornmeal; rather, he bartered to get the job done. Half of the corn that was ground into cornmeal was his, and the other half was for the person who ground the corn as the grinding fee.

Fried Herrings

Cornmeal was used for many purposes, one of which was for cooking fish. A particular kind of fish that people in rural northeastern North Carolina ate was deep fried in a cornmeal batter. The fish I am talking about is herring. Back then, you could get herring cheap, I mean really cheap, for maybe a dime a dozen or even cheaper. Sometime the fish were almost free, or the cost of a minor amount of labor, as these fish would swim up the creek and people would go right out into the Chowan River and catch them either with a fishing pole or with a net.

The real fishermen would catch up to 50 gallons of herrings, clean or gut them, and then salt them as soon as they were caught. Most people salted the herrings, as that was the best way of preserving them. Remember, there was no electricity in our neck of the woods, so no refrigerators.

When salting herrings, it was important to ensure that the fish were salted through and through. The process started by acquiring a big wooden barrel, typically a five-gallon barrel, then laying a layer of salt followed by a layer of fish and then another layer of salt and fish. This continued until the barrel was full. Some people would brine the fish, where salt water was used instead of pure salt.

Before cooking these salted herrings, one would have to soak the fish for 8 to 10 hours to reduce the saltiness of the fish somewhat, as they were really not edible if not soaked. Once soaked properly, they would be battered in cornmeal and fried hard in pork lard. It was important to fry herrings hard because they had lots and lots of bones, and when they were fried, it was commonplace to eat the bones along with the meat. It was nothing to see people eat the entire herring and just leave that spiny backbone once completed. However, frying was not the only way of cooking herrings. They could also be boiled or poached. If they happened to be cooked in this manner, it was a labor of love to eat them because it took time picking all of those tiny bones out of the meat. Occasionally, one might swallow a bone, or a bone would get stuck in your throat, and this could be extremely painful. Children had to be particularly careful when eating herrings because of all the bones, and frequently parents would pick the bones out of the fish before serving them to children.

It was very important to have the cornbread along with those herrings just in case one swallowed one of those many bones and the bone got lodged in the throat. Biting, chewing, and swallowing a piece of that cornbread was probably the number one way of dislodging a bone. Cornbread and fried fish were good eating and could be eaten for any meal—breakfast, lunch, or dinner.

Making and frying cornbread was a relatively simple process, and at its simplest would require only water and cornmeal, but it would be a little more flavorful if an egg or two was used with a little salt, water, and of course the cornmeal. The mixture would then be made into patties and fried. The patties would be about the size of a small pancake, three to four inches in diameter, and this pancake would be fried again in pork fat or lard. Once cooked, these patties would last a lifetime it seemed, as they could be stored in the cupboard for a day or two. They might become hard, but they were still edible.

Another way of making cornbread, which some people refer to as cake cornbread, was to use the ingredients as noted above but buttermilk would be used instead of water, baking powder and baking soda would be needed, and the lard/pork grease would be integrated into this mix. Instead of frying the cornbread, it would be put in a pan and cooked in the oven of that old wood stove.

I mentioned earlier that biscuits were a staple to our diet. Everyone knows that butter is a natural complement to biscuits. Where do you think we got the butter? I'll give you a hint: we didn't have a local 7-Eleven, Safeway, Food Lion, Whole Foods store, or anywhere to buy it from—we had to make our own butter. The first step involved in making butter would be to go out to the barn and milk one of the cows. My dad was sure to maintain a cow even after he stopped farming. We never slaughtered our cows. They were used primarily for milk, but they also became our pets.

When one milks a cow, the cream automatically comes up to the top of whatever container catches the milk—usually a bucket. Frequently the milk is allowed to sit overnight. The natural process is for the cream to separate from the rest of the milk. Once it separates, we—my mama, Bob, or I—would skim cream off the top. We would then put the cream in a jar and let it set.

When making the butter in the wintertime, we would sit inside by the fire. We didn't have a radio, so we didn't have anything else to do. Shaking the cream to make butter was just a leisurely activity. We could tell when it started turning into buttermilk and butter because it would begin to stick to the inside of the jar. At this point, it was almost ready.

Sometimes you would just let the milk stand until it soured or turned to clabber. When it solidified or semi-solidified, it was edible as cottage cheese. We wouldn't eat it as cottage cheese unless we put sugar on it, which we did quite often.

I believe that we almost always had a deep water well in the front yard or back yard of every house we lived in. This well allowed us to preserve some perishable foods, such as butter and cheese. We would wrap these items in waxed paper, put them in a bucket, and then put the bucket in the well so that the items could keep cool, especially in the summer. Most of our meats were smoked or salted; therefore, they rarely spoiled, but again we seldom had leftovers and never had an excessive supply of food in the pantry—unless, of course, the food was canned.

On the occasion when we did have leftovers, we put it in what you might call an ice box. In the summer, there was a man who traveled the Hertford County circuit farming community. This guy was called the ice man (not to be confused with George Gervin the basketball great). He had these large blocks of ice, maybe 25 to 50 pounds, I don't really know. What I do know is that my mama would buy a block of ice, wrap it in burlap a couple of times, and put it in the fire place. Yes, we had a crude ice box, even though we didn't have electricity. The ice would last a couple of days until the ice man came around again.

Salting and Smoking Meats

Salting and/or smoking meats and fish had a dual purpose. One was for preservation or to inhibit bacterial growth, and the second was to enhance the meats' flavor. The salting process was relatively simple and was accomplished by liberally coating a piece of meat with salt, packing it tightly in salt, and then wrapping it in a moisture-proof piece of paper/cloth and storing it in a dark dry area.

The process for smoking a piece of meat, on the other hand, included first selecting the piece of meat to be smoked, such as a pork ham. The item would then be hung in the rafters of the smoke house and exposed to smoke from burning or smoldering wood. Different types of wood would add different flavors to the meat. In our neck of the woods, wood such as hickory, oak, maple; or wood from fruit trees, such as apple, cherry, and plum trees was used. The heat couldn't be too high; if so, it would cook the meat, and we didn't want it cooked, we wanted it preserved. The meat had to be slowly smoked, often requiring days. Fish could be smoked in the same manner. Smoking meats, like cooking molasses, required attention to detail.

Before smoking or salting a piece of meat, the animal from which the selected item was to come had to be slaughtered and butchered. The animal I most often witnessed killed was the pig. Pigs are pretty fast-growing animals. For example, a pig born in the spring would likely be ready for slaughter that same fall or winter at the weight of 200 pounds or so. I think that my granddad and uncles bought piglets and fed them for slaughter. They will eat almost anything and were typically fed scraps from the dinner table, corn, and probably some store-bought protein mix.

Butchering day typically started at dawn and was a family activity. Large cast iron pots would be filled with water, and the water was brought to a boil on an open fire. My uncles were pretty brutal when it came to killing hogs, as were most farmers of the time. I've seen them hit the hog in the head with a sledgehammer or shoot the animal with a 22-caliber rifle from pretty close range. Shortly after killing the hog, its throat was cut so that the blood could drain. The quality of the meat was reportedly enhanced the sooner the blood was drained from the body. The carcass was then strung up, the organs separated and cleaned, and then put into a boiling barrel of water for hair removal before being butchered. The women were responsible for cleaning the organs, and I remember the care they took cleaning the dirtier organs, like the intestines, chitterlings. I also remember the skin being fried for crackling and much of the fat being cooked and melted into lard or grease.

My mother was particularly partial to mutton or sheep meat, and my granddad or the boys regularly slaughtered these animals in a manner similar to the one described above.

Because of Granddad's abundance of cattle, we were able to eat mutton on a regular basis, as he ensured that we kept a ready supply of mutton, pork, and beef.

Although we ate mutton, beef, and pork on a regular basis, the main staple to our diet was chicken, which we ate at least weekly if not more frequently, and almost always for Sunday dinner. The process of preparing a chicken for a meal is much different from what you might expect, as again we never bought a chicken from a market. Today in the United States, I imagine that 90% of the chickens cooked come as store-bought ready for cooking. You see, if we were to have chicken, we had to kill the chickens we ate. We always wanted the chickens we ate to be clean on the inside, because chickens would eat anything, especially worms. So, before we killed a chicken, we would take it off the yard and keep it off the yard for a few days. After a few days, when it came time for killing the chicken, we did so by chopping off its head—but we had to be really careful because after a chicken had its head chopped off, by reflex, the chicken would run around the yard flapping its wings for maybe a minute or so, splattering blood everywhere before it died. Sometimes, instead of chopping off the chicken's head, we would grab the chicken by the head and whip the body in a circle, breaking its neck.

There was another fowl similar to a chicken that we ate. It was a guinea, a bird that looks somewhat like a chicken, is about the same size as a chicken, but it has a more colorful head and no feathers. This bird is an insect and seed-eating, ground-nesting bird resembling a partridge. Guinea fowl meat is drier and leaner than chicken meat and has a gamey flavor. Not only did we eat guinea fowl but we also ate their eggs, which in my mind was not significantly different from chicken eggs. Since the guinea were so similar to a chicken, we killed them in a similar manner.

And Vegetables

The guy who rented my family the house in which I grew up—from the age of 8 to 18—rented it to us for about $3.00 a month. The rent included all the land we wanted for gardening, so we always had a garden and fresh vegetables. Mom, Dad, Andrew, and I did the gardening, and we canned much of the vegetables harvested. We grew beans, collards, cabbage, corn, watermelon, tomatoes, cucumbers, and a few others. Planting, tilling the soil, and harvesting was hard work. Undeniably life in the country was hard, but it prepared me for adulthood and the Army. The food grown was intended to last for a while, all year, so we had to preserve it and canning was the method we used.

The canning process had been passed down for generations in our community, and we continued to use it. We canned almost all of the fruits and vegetables harvested. The adult women in the family—although there were also children and adolescent girls learning the art—were responsible for canning. Canning required heating vegetables/fruits sufficiently enough to destroy microorganisms, such as enzymes, yeast, molds, and bacteria that causes food to spoil.

Once heated the food was then placed in special glass jars, either pint or quart jars, with special metal lids that have rubber seals at the bottom, effectively sealing the contents in and everything else out. Canning was a process that my mother, grandmother, and the women of the time did at harvesting time, and the food preserved carried us for the next year.

The canned jars of fruit/vegetables were stored in a cool, dry place, which was best for maintaining their nutritional value. If cooked correctly, canned correctly, and stored correctly, foods would last for a year or more.

The Hunt

Bob and I contributed significantly to what the family ate. Just like most boys and men did at the time, we hunted wild game. I am not aware of any females hunting back then, and I am certain my mother, grandmother, and aunts didn't hunt; but there could have been others who did.

The family always had at least one shotgun, and I used it on a regular basis from about the age of 12 or younger. I hunted squirrels, rabbits, and wild bird, but I never did kill anything larger, like a deer. The shotgun was the most reliable weapon for hunting because one didn't need to be that accurate. We also used less accurate guns, however. When I was about 14, Bob bought a 22-caliber rifle that he and I also used. You had to practice and be patient if you wanted to bag an animal with that .22. Neither the shotgun nor the .22 rifle we used had much of a kick. They couldn't, as I was only about 12 when I started hunting. I was not large by any means and didn't have much muscle mass. The .22 forced me to become an accurate shooter.

We lived right there next to the woods, so I didn't have to go far to hunt, and although we hunted for meat for our meals, I enjoyed hunting because it was simply fun and something to do. I did most of my hunting on Saturday mornings, especially during the school year, and although hunting was important, chores always came first. I was a pretty good shot and frequently bagged rabbits and squirrels and I did my own gutting, cleaning, and skinning. Squirrels had tough hides, so it took a while to skin them, but rabbits, well, I don't see how rabbits survived in the woods. Their hides (fur and skin) are oh-so tender and soft; I would take skinning a rabbit any day to a squirrel.

Getting back to the guns we used for hunting, certainly hunting for preadolescents was no big deal. I never had to get permission to hunt, nor did I always advise my parents when I was going hunting. I just did, and they never said anything to me about it.

We also ate the occasional turtle. Jonnie Burk, an older cousin, was one of the few people I can remember who would catch turtles. I don't know that turtles are dangerous, and they are absolutely slow creatures, so I don't know why more people didn't catch them. Anyway, once a turtle was caught, it would then be put in a barrel for a couple of days before killing it for the same reason that the guinea fowl and chicken were taken off the yard only we didn't feed the turtle anything while they were in the barrel waiting to be killed.

Turtles were killed by cutting off their heads, and everyone I knew believed that the heads would live for three days after it was cut off. No one ever confirmed this, but no one ever went looking for the severed head once it was cut off either.

Turtle meat was good meat, and I can't say that it tastes like any kind of meat but turtle. Again, I wonder to this day why more people didn't eat turtle meat.

Christmas Vittles

Christmas was an anxious time for children, although we never got toys and gifts as children do today, nor was Christmas as commercialized as it is today. It couldn't be that commercialized because there were no televisions, computers, iPads, iPhones, Galaxies, or other type of mobile devices, and there were only a limited number of radios. Also, when I was a young child, the country was going through the worst depression ever, and there was an absence of disposable income. So, no, we did not get toys on Christmas, and rarely did we get toys during the year. For Christmas, we received really simple presents, such as a pair of socks. We also got a bag of goodies, edibles like oranges, apples, raisins, nuts, and candy. This was special, and we really appreciated this bag of goodies.

The Christmas meal, however, was always something special. It was pretty much like a very extraordinary Sunday dinner. I don't believe we ever had a turkey for Christmas—maybe a ham, some mutton, and of course chicken. Christmas dinners were particularly special because of the desserts—cakes and pies. Mom cooked a bunch of cakes and pies. We had two safes, or oak kitchen cabinets, where we could store food, and one safe would be full of cakes and pies, maybe four or five each.

Mom started cooking cakes a week before Christmas, as the wood stove in which she cooked was exceedingly small. The cakes would typically keep for maybe a week after Christmas and wouldn't spoil. They might get dry, but that was okay. They maintained their sweetness, I think. My dad would also cook a cake. His specialty was an apple cake, and that was the only cake he cooked all year; his cake was also out of this world.

Adjusting to Army Meals

When I went into the military, I really had to get adjusted to the military diet, especially in basic training. The food was just different from what I was used to eating at home, and I did not like it. I believe that one of the major differences was that military food was cooked in such large quantities, whereas Mama cooked for maybe five or ten at the most. Army cooks were cooking for hundreds or thousands and couldn't be expected to satisfy everyone's pallet. For sure Army food, at least initially, didn't satisfy me, but it was sustenance. I ate it, always cleaning my plate except green peppers, and didn't complain. I had been taught to eat everything on my plate as a child because we didn't have much. We had limited means of preserving what was cooked, and since I was raised during the worst depression the US had seen, we didn't have anything to waste.

In the military, we ate a lot of white potatoes with green peppers. As a matter of fact, they seemed to put green peppers in everything they cooked, and I hated green peppers. I hated the green peppers to such a degree that I would pick them out of my serving whenever time allowed, which was rare in boot camp. Since green peppers were a staple, I eventually learned to tolerate them, if not even like them, over time.

The military plays mind games with soldiers, and it seems as if one of the mind games they played, at least during basic training, was to have routine drills during the lunch or dinner hour. If there was a drill, I would grab as much food as I could because there was little to no chance that we were going back to the mess hall after a drill.

Despite eating relatively well, I probably lost a little weight when I got out of basic training, and I couldn't afford to lose too much, as I only weighed about 140 pounds when I was inducted. I stayed at that weight until I got out of the Army, which was two years, eight months, and eight days later. Over the next 18 or so years, I would eat thousands of meals in the mess hall, some hot meals in the field, and hundreds of C rations.

The military food was okay, but Mama's, Essie Nora's, and Grandma's food was great. As I think about their food today, my mouth waters.

Beginning Primer Grades at Four

I started school in either 1928 or 1929 at about the age of four. The first year I attended school didn't really count, as the teacher just allowed me to attend with other family members as a favor to my mother. School was important to my mother, even though she had little formal education. Four is young to be walking to school, but I didn't go by myself; rather, I went along with older relatives.

One of these relatives was my aunt, my father's baby sister, Martha Newsome. Martha was considerable older than I was, and although I don't really know her age, and certainly didn't know it back then, I know that she was in elementary school—maybe in the sixth or seventh grade. She was a valuable resource (refuge) for me, as I looked up to her. In school, I was glad that I got an opportunity to see her frequently.

It may seem odd today to say that she was maybe six grades ahead of me, and I saw her often, but back then that didn't mean much because there were only two classrooms in the entire school. I am sure you have probably heard of a one-room school. Well, the school we attended, the Cotton School, was a two-room school. In this school, the little kids were in one classroom, and I think that the grades in the class I attended ranged from what we would call kindergarten today to the fifth grade. The older kids, or kids in the junior high grades six and seven, were in the other classroom. Martha was in the other classroom with the bigger and older children.

The Cotton School was a small building on what is called the Little California Road. It is between Winton and Ahoskie in a little junction on the Murfreesboro Highway. It is in a location about a half-mile from Mount Mariah Church, the church my family and I attended for a while, and the church where I was first baptized. As of this writing, the Cotton School is still standing in its original location; however, you might not be able to see it from the highway because it has bushes and trees growing up all around it.

Martha, Jessie, and I walked together the half or maybe full mile from our house on my grandfather's farm. I don't know why the teacher allowed me to attend school, but I was well behaved and was never a behavior or management problem. If I had been, I am sure that the teacher would not have allowed me to stay in class. As mentioned before, I did suffer from a seizure disorder as a child, and this could have derailed my first year in school, but it didn't, and the disorder went away as I approached high school. Nonetheless, the arrangement with me going to school worked out well for my mother, as she didn't have to keep me at home when she was busy working.

The way I behaved in school, where I got along well with everyone, was not consistent with my behavior at home. My relationship with Mom can probably best be described as contentious. I guess she was overly protective, and I needed my space.

At any rate, as I look back on my first year of schooling, the arrangement may have been more akin to babysitting as opposed to me being fully engaged in the academic process. But of course, I was eager to please and have always been quietly competitive, so I suspect that I learned a thing or two. Whether I learned anything or not, I was happy that first year in school. After all, there would have been little for me to do if I'd remained at home alone.

My real academic training began at the age of five. At this age, I was a real student and fully participated in all classroom activities. I was in what might be called kindergarten today, but back then the first year of schooling was called the primer grade. The primer grade was the grade that children attended prior to the first grade—so they called that the primer. In my second year of school, Bob walked with me, Jessie, and Martha. Bob also started school for the first time that year, and the two of us were in the same grade, in the same class, and with the same teachers until the sixth grade. I failed the sixth grade, so Bob left me and thus graduated a year before me. Bob was several years older than me, so he should have graduated before me; it was not his fault that he had been unable to begin school until the age of eight or so.

Bob and I attended the Cotton School until I was in the second or third grade, and we had a different teacher each year. I remember vividly the teacher I had in the second grade. In my mind, she was a real witch. Her name may have been Ms. Watford, but I am not exactly sure. As I think back to the second grade, what comes to my mind is that the teacher was a real bully. I mean, she was just mean and hateful (this language certainly makes me feel like I am back in the second grade at the age of six). She probably wasn't all that bad, but I didn't see any good in her. From what I remember, Ms. Watford would beat this one girl, Nancellia, almost daily. Nancellia was probably in the fourth or fifth grade. From what I could see, she would beat her for no reason at all. At the age of six, and even looking back today, the only reason I could see for the mistreatment was that Ms. Watford was just evil.

I would guess that this poor girl had no one to advocate for her because her mother was sick and confined to bed, so she couldn't go to school to defend her daughter. The girl's father was a minister, or what we used to call a jack legged preacher. A lot of black men had the title of preacher back then and preached in various locations. I believe that he could have taken up his daughter's cause, but even he did not defend her. This may have been a sign of the times, where the teacher was always right.

To my knowledge, the year she was so badly mistreated was her last year in that class, so she probably moved over to the next class. I believe that she still lives somewhere in Ahoskie, and some of her daughters were in school at Elizabeth City State University with my oldest two sons, Edward and Marcus. Without a doubt, this girl valued education, as she made sure her daughters went on to not only graduate from high school but also college. In a strange twist of fate, I believe that those two daughters became school teachers.

Although we have not maintained a close relationship, I have tracked her life and believe that she had a number of children, losing a son in an automobile accident. When Nancellia was growing up, she and her family always lived fairly close to my folks. As a matter of fact, at one point in time, she and her family lived next door to my uncle Reddick, my father's oldest brother, in Mapleton, which is outside of Murfreesboro.

Getting back to Ms. Watford, I don't believe that there was one student in the entire school that liked her. The older students, being more mature, disliked her so much that as I remember, they developed a plot to band together and were going to teach her a lesson by beating her up. I don't know what prevented them from revolting and assaulting Ms. Watford, but I would have been on their side. Even today, I feel as if it would have been justified. There I go again, regressing back to the age of six. Of course, this type of violence would have been wrong.

On the other hand, every student in the entire school loved and admired Ms. Lue Brown, who taught the upper level students, the sixth- and seventh-grade classroom. This teacher was extremely nice, caring, easy going, and had no flaws in our eyes.

Bob, my brother, had a confrontation and stood up to Ms. Watson one day. He was mild-mannered and comfortable with who he was, so he was seldom challenged; but when he was, he rarely backed down.

One day, Bob was sitting in class, and his mind must have been drifting somewhere that only he knows—probably like all elementary age students do and something I imagine he has done a thousand times before. On this particular occasion, he was lightly drumming on his desk, and Ms. Watford told him to stop that banging. Well, he kept on drumming. Maybe he wasn't so meek and was antsy for a fight/confrontation. Anyway, Ms. Watford came back there and grabbed him. He wiggled free and grabbed her right back. He then went to the back of the class and into the coat room, got a piece of wood, and threatened to hit her with it.

Well, of course she was much larger and was able to take the log away from him. She was able to de-escalate the situation to the point where he calmed down and was able to stay in school. In this day and age, I am sure he would have been suspended or even expelled.

Wood and logs were very prevalent in the school back then, year round, because the school was heated by wood. Teachers also served dual roles: they were both teacher and school cooks. They cooked lunch using wood stoves for all of the students in school. Many of the students were from poor families, and this may have been one of the few meals they got.

The day after the event involving Bob and Ms. Watford, Ms. Katie (I have forgotten her last name), a senior school administrator for the African American schools in our county and my family's former neighbor, came to the school to investigate the incident. How she got the news about the incident we will never know; possibly it was the upper grade teacher. Upon arrival to the school, she called all of the children and teachers into one of the schoolrooms, and then she began asking the students about the scuffle between Bob and Ms. Watford. No one volunteered anything because they liked Bob and didn't like Ms. Watford. I guess they had a no snitching rule back then, too, except not everyone was following the rule. Eventually, one girl got up the gumption to volunteer and tell what had occurred. Once Bob was identified, Ms. Katie asked him to come up before the class. She then told him to get on his knees and apologize to Ms. Watford. Andrew was much calmer by then and complied with the administrator's request.

After school that day, the assistant superintendent stopped by our house on the way back to town and had a discussion with my mother, who really loved Bob as much if not more than me. (No, she really, really loved me, too.) Anyway, after that incident, the students didn't have any more problems with Ms. Watford because I think she got the hint, if not the word, that she wasn't welcome out there or in the community. Bob became the school's hero.

In addition to the two classrooms, there was also a small kitchen. Although the menu was slim, all of the students looked forward to lunch. Beans are the only thing I can ever remember being served, but they were sooo good, satisfying, and we were always anxious to eat those beans. I believe that the county, state, or some other government agency supplied the beans. Even today, I can remember seeing that big pot of beans on the wooden stove and smelling the sweet, salty smell of them, yum yum. The only place we were ever provided lunch was at the Cotton School.

Although there were no lunches served at the other schools I attended, at C. S. Brown they had a canteen where we could buy snacks. At C. S. Brown, all of the girls had to complete a home economics class before they graduated, and part of the course required them to cook. Most of the girls had learned to cook at home under their mothers' or grandmothers' tutelage, so they were fairly good cooks. In any case, me and a lot of the guys would make sure that we were nearby the class when the girls were cooking so that we could sample their meals.

When I transferred to Pleasant Plains School, since lunch was not provided, we had to bring our own or go hungry. I normally brought my lunch in a little tin lunch box. It wasn't a store-bought lunch box, but it was my lunch box nevertheless, and it was special. My parents, like many people of the time, bought lard in little buckets/tins, and many of my classmates used these tins for lunch boxes.

Lard is simply pig fat that is boiled in water or steamed at a high temperature, and the lard, which is insoluble in water, is skimmed off the surface of the mixture, and it is separated. It was commonly used in many cuisines as a cooking fat or shortening. Lard was used as a shortening for frying meats and for baking almost exclusively when I was growing up. Today, vegetable or olive oil is often used because of the unhealthy effects of lard on the body. The lard would come in quart-size tins, and it was these containers that the children broke out at lunchtime.

On the other hand, my lunch box was much more special. My granddad used to smoke pipes, and the tobacco for the pipes came in big tins—eight inches long, four or five inches wide. This is what I had for a lunch box, and it was special because it came from my granddad. I was special to my granddad, and my granddad was special to me. I can't remember the type of tobacco that came in the container, but I can remember clearly that it had a picture of George Washington on the box.

My mother generally packed our lunch, and it typically consisted of a fried egg. We had lots of eggs around the house because we raised chickens and maybe harvested a dozen eggs a week. Bob and I probably also had fatback and a biscuit for lunch. Fatback is a cut of meat from domesticated pigs. It is typically the layer of meat just under the skin of the back of the hog, with or without the skin. It is similar to a piece of bacon but thicker and has a much large collection of fat than does traditional bacon.

The biscuits were cooked from scratch, and they were the most wonderful biscuits in the world. I have eaten biscuits all over the world but have found none to be as tasty as my mother's.

Most children packed similar meals, although some might have a biscuit with molasses, some might only have a biscuit, while others had no lunch at all.

Bob and I transition from the Cotton School to the Pleasant Plains School when we were in the third grade. We attended the Pleasant Plains School for grades three, four, and five, for a total of three years. This school was a little larger than the Cotton School. To the best of my recollection, it had three classrooms and three teachers. One of the teachers lived right across the road from the school. Another teacher lived a little further down on Highway 13, in the cross, from where Branches Auto Dealership stands today. The third teacher, I think, lived somewhere in Union maybe about five or ten miles away.

Viola Chavis was one of the teachers, and I would describe her as a very excellent teacher. Audale Garrett taught us when we were in the fifth grade at Pleasant Plains, and then I remember another teacher at the time, a Ms. Hall, but I don't remember what grade she taught. All of the teachers at both the Cotton and Pleasant Plains schools were women.

One of the things in particular that I remember from the Pleasant Plains school was getting into one fight there. I don't really know what started the fight. Maybe I was just a bit meaner than the other kid and just wanted to showboat. This kid's name was Anthony, and at recess one day, I had set my mind that I was going to get him. For some reason, I couldn't catch up with him, as it seemed that every time he saw me coming after him, he would run back into the school. He knew that I was out to get him.

After a bit of this cat and mouse chasing, some of my buddies decided to help me corner him. They told me that they would catch him after school and hold him until I arrived so that I could beat him up. I don't think that they caught him that day, so I didn't get a chance to fight him and this only made me more angry. I did finally catch up with him one day as I happened to see him standing outside in front of the school and knew that if he saw me, he would step back in the building. So, on this particular day, I went all the way around the building, came up behind him, and just hauled off and punched him. He ran back in to the school, so I didn't get to fight him the way I wanted, but I was satisfied, and our feud ended.

Albert Lawrence was in my class, as was his brother and Robert. There was another brother, too, but I can't recall his name. Their father was a guy who I thought was kinda weird. He didn't like the Newsomes, none of them, so if you had the Newsome name, he wouldn't speak to you. His name was

Oga Lawrence, and his wife was Lucy. She was a very sweet and friendly lady, Oga on the other hand would come down the street riding in his mule-driven cart, pass the house, and look the other way. The Newsomes were kinda meddlesome themselves, and when they saw Old Oga, they would always speak to him anyway. "Hey, Old Oga," and he would just look the other way. He just wouldn't speak to a Newsome, and I have no idea why; his kids would play with us, but Oga had no use for us.

I suspect that the feud started long ago between him and my granddad, who was probably hardheaded and stubborn also. I can remember my granddad being a cantankerous old guy, and I am sure he insulted Oga about something, so Oga didn't want to have anything to do with anybody who was a Newsome.

Somewhere around 1933, the county began closing down some of its elementary schools, and this chain of events impacted the Pleasant Plains School. The Pleasant Plains School was reduced from a seven grades school to a five grades school, and the fifth grade became the senior-most grade at the school. In this shuffle, I was forced to transition from the Pleasant Plains School to a school in Winton.

When I first began attending this school, it was named the Winton School. Later, before I graduated, the name was changed to the Waters Training School, and a few years after that, the name was changed again to Calvin S. Brown High School. This was shortened to C. S. Brown by most attendees, graduates, rival schools, and people living in the area.

Not long after the Chowan Academy (Winton School) became the C. S. Brown High School, all of the feeder schools in the area—to include elementary and junior high schools—consolidated, and all children in the area were assigned to attend C. S. Brown High School. C. S. Brown still stands today and is actually on the same site with two or its original buildings. In the main building, they still have local meetings and various other functions or ceremonies. One of the original buildings on campus was destroyed by fire. All I know about the fire is that one day, when the bus arrived at the school, the building was no longer there. The only thing that was left were a lot of ashes. I think that that was my last year at C. S. Brown, and we never found out the cause of the fire.

Calvin S. Brown was the founder of C. S. Brown School, and his wife, daughter, and granddaughter taught me. Certainly, you can say that the Browns were a family of educators.

Calvin S. Brown was an educator, editor, minister, and advisor. He was raised by farmers and brought up in poverty. He was educated at Freedman's Aid Society School and obtained his undergraduate degree from Shaw University in Raleigh. Upon graduation, he assumed the pastorate of Pleasant Plains Baptist Church in Pleasant Plains, North Carolina and later founded the all-black Chowan Academy, which later became Waters Training School, and finally Calvin S. Brown High School. C. S. Brown was one of the few African Americans at the time to travel extensively throughout the United States, Europe, and Africa.

I don't know that school back in my day was much different from school today. We had homework on a regular basis; however, the code of conduct might have been different because we had corporal punishment. My family didn't have electricity, and very few people I knew did, so at night,

I imagine that most children like Bob and myself studied by candlelight. Back in my day, as it is today, not everyone passed every year from grade to grade. Indeed, I failed the sixth grade, and I don't mind telling anyone this. The reason I failed is because I simply didn't do my work sufficiently to pass. That's the usual reason for failing, no excuses. There were other students who failed, but that does not minimize the fact that I failed, and I would be lying if I said I was the best student in the class and the teacher didn't have just cause for holding me back.

The school founder's daughter, Flora Brown Collins, was the teacher who failed me. In my opinion, she really wasn't a good teacher, but again that is not the reason I failed. She didn't do a whole lot of teaching. As I remember it she would come into class, write a bunch of stuff on the blackboard, get her purse, stick it under her arm, and walk out. We didn't know where she went. I was in the class of Ms. Brown Collins for two years the year I failed and the year after; hopefully, I was a little smarter the second time around.

I do remember that my uncle died that year. We called him Bayboy and he had been sick for a while. I don't know what the cause of his death was, but I do know that back in those days, it was rare for a black person to go see and/or be treated by a doctor, and even rarer for a black person to be hospitalized.

Although I failed the sixth grade, it wasn't because I was a poor math student. I was actually a superior math student. I remember way back to the Cotton School when I first started school and had that "bad" teacher. She used to put math problems on the chalkboard, and she would make a stair step, and each step would have a problem. She would call on each student to go up to the board and solve a given problem. When the student got to a problem he or she couldn't solve, the teacher would draw a little figure, and the figure would be falling off the step. I never ever fell off any of the steps and would frequently climb all the way up to the top of the steps. I never had any problem with math throughout school. Math was always my favorite subject it just came naturally, and I always got high grades. I can remember back to high school when the girls got angry at the math teachers for giving the boys higher grades than the girls. They always left me out of this debate, making it clear that they were not talking about Edward. Part of the reason they were not talking about Edward was because, me Edward, was their math lifeline and always helped them with their assignments.

My math skills would help me later in life when I attended radar repair school. Half the class washed out in the first week because of the math-intensive curriculum. Math was my favorite subject, followed by chemistry as a close second, and thus my assignment to radar repair school. Although there were few who could compete with me in math, my brother was a better all-around student and made much better grades than I did. I have always thought that Bob was much more intelligent. I know that he was more mature and wiser than I.

I was in the first graduating class at C. S. Brown High School in 1943. There were 48 or 50 people in the graduating class. Only seven or eight were boys—all the rest were girls. I was elected the class president, and although I didn't want the position, my fellow students voted me in, and I reluctantly I accepted. This is what happened, I knew that the election was coming up and had heard that my classmates wanted to elect me as president, so on election day, I tried to get lost. I even skipped class. My classmates were having none of this and sent a posse out after me; they found me and elected me anyway, despite my reluctance.

My vice president that year was Evelyn Gasden, who became a senior administrator at Bennett College. Bennett College which opened in 1873, when seventy African American women and men began gathering for primary and secondary studies in the basement of Warnersville Methodist Episcopal Church in Greensboro, North Carolina. It likely would not have opened if it were not for white northern philanthropists who contributed tremendously to the school. In 1926, Bennett College, a private, four-year, historically black liberal arts college became an all-women's college and today it still stands as an all-women's college. John Manley, who later became a preacher, was the valedictorian of my senior class; Manley went on to attend and graduate from Shaw University.

In addition to being elected class president, I was voted the best dressed male of my graduating class. Throughout high school myself, Bob, and all the boys wore neckties. I don't know if it was a rule or not, but everyone did.

Now C. S. Brown was a rural school, but the kids with whom I graduated were successful in different ways. Ernest Simmons of Harrellsville, North Carolina became a doctor. Ernest Simmons' brother ran the local credit union in Ahoskie. John Manley became a minister in Raleigh. One of my classmates, who currently lives in Como, became a nurse. Rochell Vann was four years ahead of me at the Waters

Training School, after graduation he became a teacher at C. S. Brown before later teaching and working in an administrative capacity at Elizabeth State University. Evelyn Gasden's brother worked with the Agriculture Department in Washington, DC. Evelyn Gasden's youngest brother became a principal here in Hertford County. His name was Richard Gasden, and I think that he died in 2008.

Like me, I believe most fled the rural community and farms as soon as they got the opportunity. Certainly, that is one of the reasons I joined the military.

At least two of my classmates, in addition to me, went into the military. T. S. Britt went into the US Navy, and his wife still lives in Poticassy about eight miles from where we currently live in Ahoskie. Thomas Britt (T. S. Britt) got drafted out of high school and wasn't able to get a deferment. After T. S. got out of the military, he started an auto mechanics business in Norfolk, Virginia. As luck would have it, or the lack of luck you might say, his place of business burned down, so he moved up to Washington, DC and became a preacher.

Two of my wife's brothers also got drafted into the military at about the same time. Turner Lee (T. L.) Holloman became a truck driver in Europe, and he swears that that was the most dangerous job in the US Army. William was also drafted and became a cook in the US Navy.

I imagine that some of the students ahead of me at C. S. Brown, and some after me probably, also went into the military because of World War II (WWII), where the federal government was drafting everyone they could. Remember, in my graduating class, there were only seven or eight boys; three went into the military. There are a number of other fellow graduates whom I remember, but I can't say that I have kept in touch with them. They would be Bynum Vann, Mason Watson (who I understand drowned not long after graduation), Sam Eley (who I think also was called up for the military), Sadie White, Gertrude Everett, Mabel Reynolds, Pauline Newsome, Irene Bynum, Holly Jenkins, Benjamin Gadsen, and Emma Ruffin.

Although school was important to me, I had a burning desire to get away from home and wanted to go into the Civilian Conservation Corps a year before I graduated. They were paying, as much or more than the Army was paying, and I really wanted to get away. College wasn't something that was on my mind. It wasn't that I didn't like school it just seemed that getting a diploma back then didn't have the value that it has now because a lot of people didn't have one. The Civilian Conservation Corps (CCC) was a public work relief program, which began in 1933 for the unemployed or unmarried as part of the New Deal signed by Franklin D. Roosevelt. The CCC provided unskilled manual labor jobs related to conservation and development of natural resources, such as working on bridges, transportation, erosion control, flood control, forest protection, landscape, recreation, and wildlife. Mama insisted that I stay in school, which I did, and it was probably for the best.

Like some of my cohorts I would like to think that I also had an impressive career. There were no special highlights, but I devoted my life to my family. All of my children have college degrees, and three have doctorate degrees. I was, I believe, the first African American to work on the nuclear bomb, as I never saw another black person working on the bomb in my tenure with nuclear bomb units. Upon retiring from the Army, I obtained a job working for the US Postal Service, retiring on my 60th birthday.

Teachers who left an impression upon me included Ms. Watford, C. S. Brown's daughter Flora Brown-Collin, and Flora's daughter Amaza Collins-Reed. C. S. Brown's granddaughter taught me English and literature in high school. My favorite teacher was Ester Britt, my science teacher. However, Dennis McKaskell and Howard Bond, who taught algebra, geometry, and chemistry, were teachers I admired and liked a lot. Since I liked and was good at math, they were good to me. Dennis would also mentor us regarding life skills when it rained and we were prevented from going outside. Everyone liked Dennis.

There was another teacher who never taught at a school that I attended, and with whom I had very limited interactions, but who nevertheless significantly impacted my life. This lady taught in Harrisville, and she stayed in Harrisville during the week. She lived right behind us and subscribed to the local newspaper; so, when the paper came out, it was placed in her paper box. I would go get her paper, read it, and return it to her box before she returned home on the weekend. Her newspaper is where I got my current events to present in school. That was probably two or three years before I graduated from high school. I needed the current events for school, so I had to read the newspaper.

Many kids didn't have access to any media, and this made for very limited access to current events. I don't think that the teacher knew I was reading her paper; I was just borrowing it. People were more willing to loan stuff back then than they are now. Even so, it was wrong, and I would not have permitted my children to engage in similar behavior.

People tell all sorts of stories about school 50 or 60 years ago. One that you hear all the time is that we walked miles and miles to school, but I never did. I walked maybe a mile to the first two schools I attended, the Cotton School and Pleasant Plains School, but schools were consolidated after the fifth grade, and from that point on, I road buses to school. As a matter of fact, my Essie Nora's eldest brother, Turner (T. L.), was one our bus drivers.

The Cotton School, Pleasant Plains School, Waters Training School, and C. S. Brown were all Rosenwald Schools. Rosenwald Schools was the name applied to over five thousand schools, shops, and teachers' homes in the United States, which were built primarily for the purpose of educating African Americans in the early 20th century. The need arose because of the chronic underfunding of public education for African American children by white legislators in the South. If African American students were to be educated, white legislators were determined that they would be educated in underfunded, segregated schools. Thousands of children would never have been educated except for philanthropists like Julius Rosenwald. Julius Rosenwald was an American clothier who became part owner and president of Sears Roebuck and Company and was the founder of The Rosenwald Fund, through which he contributed seed money for many of the schools later to become known as the Rosenwald Schools.

To promote collaboration between white and black citizens, Rosenwald required communities to commit public funds to the schools, as well as to contribute additional cash donations. African American rural communities raised millions of dollars across the South to fund better education for their children. Despite Rosenwald matching donations toward the construction of black schools, by the mid-1930s, white schools in the South were worth, per student, over five times what black schools were worth per student, and these predominately white schools were primarily funded through public coffers, as mandated through the legislature.

Julius Rosenwald and his family established the Rosenwald Fund in 1917 for "the well-being of mankind." The school-building program was one of the largest programs administered by the Rosenwald Fund. Using state-of-the-art architectural plans designed by professors at Tuskegee Institute, an Historically Black College University (HBCU), the Fund spent more than four million dollars to build 4,977 schools, 217 teachers' homes, and 163 shop buildings in 883 counties across 15 states, from Maryland to Texas. The $4 million in 1917 would be valued at approximately $80 million today.

By 1932, the facilities would accommodate one-third of all African American children in Southern schools. Who knows where we would be today without the Rosenwald Funds.

My school class – I am third from the left on the bottom row

Just Country Life

Back in the 1930s and '40s, we had no computers, laptops, or anything like that, so we spent much more time interacting with others or outside engaging in mostly social activities. Our games were pretty simple. One of the games I played as a child was marbles. Marbles was a game that used smooth, round pieces of glass, maybe a third of an inch or a half-inch in diameter. A circle would be drawn in the dirt on the ground, about 12 to 18 inches in diameter, and each player would place the same number of marbles in the circle. Two or more players would drop a single marble, which would be their shooter marble, on the outside of the circle, and the player with the marble landing closest to the circle would shoot first. Each player then, in turn, would shoot their shooter marble at one of the marbles in the circle, attempting to knock that marble out of the circle. If successful, that person would continue to shoot until he missed, and then it was the next person's turn. Each marble captured belonged to the person who knocked it out of the circle.

Playing marbles was somewhat like playing pool—where you put English on the marbles to make them go where you wanted them to go after striking another marble. The goal of the game was to acquire as many marbles as possible and to this end, some people would leave with a pocket/bag full of marbles. Another might leave with only their shooter. Years later, I would think about this game of winners and losers when seeing soldiers leave poker games on payday with no money left for the month and others having just added significantly to their accounts.

Another simple game that we children played was checkers. Everyone played checkers, even the elderly. This game is so common even today that it needs no explanation.

The card game I most enjoyed playing, and thus played the most, was bid whist, which I initially played as a child and played well into adulthood. Bid whist was one of two card games I played when living in Germany with other GIs, that other game was pinochle.

As a child we also played stickball, and frequently we would go to the ball park and watch baseball games. No, we didn't go to Yankee Park or the Cubs or anywhere like that; we watched games at little fields in the community, where the neighborhood adults played ball. Also in the summer, sometimes we would go out to the filling station—what today might be called a gas station because it had gas pumps. We didn't go to get gas for a car. We didn't have one. We went to socialize, the filling station was multiple-purposed, as it also served as the local grocery store. In our neck of the woods, there were two filling stations within walking distance of my house. Again, just walking to the filling station was important to us, as it gave us something to do.

I remember that everyone was like family back in those days, and one of our filling stations owners was murdered by a white man for no reason at all. The owner was Bud Keene, who had a brother nicknamed Billy Boy. Bud was a funny, very likable guy who had his ways, but he was very "law-abiding." He sold beer legally in dry Hertford County. The county didn't sell alcohol, but beer was legal. If Bud thought that you had had too much to drink, he would not sell you anymore. Well, one night, these two white guys came into the store drunk wanting to buy some beer, and Bud refused to sell it to them. They became irate, telling Bud that he would not live to see the New Year in. Just before Christmas of that year, Billy Boy was sitting on a soda crate. Back in those days, soda pop came in bottles, and the bottles were delivered to merchants in a wooden crate, which would hold four cartons of six sodas, or 24 individual bottles of soda. The crates were sturdy, and people often used them to sit on, especially when playing checkers. So, Billy Boy was sitting on the crate next to the heater, and Bud was sitting on the bar, and these two white men, to whom Bud refused to sell beer earlier in the year, came in the store—one from each of the two entrances. One had a double barrel shotgun and shot Bud in the gut, knocking him off his seat. The first shot didn't kill him, so Bud was crawling behind the counter to get his gun and had to crawl past an open area, when the murderers shot him again with the second barrel of the shotgun, killing him.

Neither of the white men attempted to harm Billy Boy sitting on the soda crate, and it was Billy Boy who testified in court against the murderers. The murderer got eight years for the murder, and his accomplice got something less. Billy Boy ran the store after Bud was murdered.

Bud was a fine, friendly gentleman who had three sisters and a brother who lived in a log cabin not far from the store. After Bud's murder, going to that store never seemed the same for me, even though Billy Boy, a local, someone who was always at the store anyway, was the proprietor.

Fishing with Grandma

Country living without electricity simply meant that we found things to occupy our time that didn't require electricity. In the summer, one of our favorite pastimes, other than baseball, and certainly the thing that I enjoyed doing most with my grandmother was fishing. My grandmother Mary loved to fish, and she would take me fishing on a regular basis several times weekly. We didn't go to school during the summer, so I had extra time on my hands then.

We primarily fished in the Potecasi Creek. Sometimes it was just me, and sometimes there was a whole group of us fishing. There might be Ernest, Annie, Martha, Jonnie, my dad, and my mom.

We never went to the market to purchase a store-bought fishing rod. We made our rods out of different materials for different types of fish. We used materials commonly found around the house, along with branches and reeds for our fishing equipment. We always had corks around the house, as almost everything we bought that came in a bottle used corks to keep the liquid in. We used the corks for floats, and of course we had different sized corks for different sized floats. The corks allowed our hooks to be suspended in the water without sinking. The poles were frequently composed of wood or strong tree branches for the larger fish, and reeds made from sugarcane and such for smaller fish.

Our typical catch from the Potecasi Creek included perch, catfish, blackfish (a really dark-red fish), and something we caught what we called chubs, which I think were bigmouth bass. We also caught the occasional eel, which we would either throw back in the creek or use for bait.

In order to get to the creek, we had to walk through the woods, where we ran across the occasional snake. Sometimes we encountered water moccasins. I remember as clearly as day one occasion where we were headed back home from fishing and a black snake crossed the path behind us. I said I was going to get that snake and went to get a stick. When I went back to kill the snake, instead of it moving away, the snake moved towards me. Of course, I retreated, and the snake retreated. Once the snake retreated, I went back to get it with my stick, and again instead of going in the opposite direction, it moved in my direction again. We did this dance two or three times, and I decided to let it be.

The snake then crawled up a tree and stretched out on a branch. I went home to get the shotgun because I was not going to let that snake outwit me. I had to best the snake, but in the long run, it did outwit me. When I got back to the tree, the snake was gone.

On another occasion, when going to or coming from the creek, there was a storm with lightning, which occurred fairly frequently in the summer. On this particular occasion, the lightning was particularly brutal, so my grandmother and I took shelter in a large tree that had been hollowed out some at the base. We stayed there until the storm passed, and then we proceeded home as usual.

When we fished it was for sport, recreation, but also vittles, and whatever we caught was quickly cleaned, cooked, and eaten.

Fishing became a lifelong passion of mine. After retiring from the military, while living in Portsmouth, Essie Nora and I would frequently visit Harrison's Pier in the Ocean View section of Norfolk, or one of the piers in Virginia Beach, where we would fish for hours on summer evenings.

My Passion—Baseball

Every town, city, or locality in rural North Carolina had a baseball team back in those days, and it was the number one summer pastime. My dad was the manager of our local team as far back as I can remember—back to when I was maybe four or five years old. Dad would recruit the guys in the neighborhood to play ball for his team. Some came as far as Union and St. John, maybe five miles one way.

This was a tight group, and even in the wintertime they found reasons to get together. In the winter, on weekends, they hunted together and eventually formed a hunting club.

In the summertime, there was a field right off what is called Little California, going to the big Mary Road. Later, the field that we used was right behind C. S. Brown High School. These were our home locations, but the team also traveled (even though the owner really didn't like to travel). Mom, Bob, and I always traveled with the team.

Wherever we played, there was always a pretty good crowd. There always seemed to be more children than adults, but there were a good number of adults, including women. My mom ran a concession stand where she sold ice cream and candy. She would get a box of ice, a lard can, and a big tin tub. She would put the lard can in the tub surrounded by ice. Inside the lard can, she added a little salt and ice cream batter, then shook the lard can until she had ice cream.

Mom got the candy from vendors that traveled the countryside selling candy. She would simply markup whatever candy she bought so that she could make a profit. I was always able to eat all the ice cream I wanted—not so with the candy, but I got enough candy also.

As mentioned, most of the players on the team were local players. I also got a chance to play for my dad's team, but it wasn't until after I got out of the Army in 1946. I was a pretty good player, playing both first base and pitcher.

The best team in the area at the time was the Chowan Bees, name after the Chowan River in Hertford County. Then there was a team called the Homestead, and also teams from the Negro National League that we played. The catcher of the Bees, a guy by the name of Joe Lee Windborne, actually made one of Negro National League teams. Other players on the Bees team were Possi (Elber Archer), Wilert Archer, Jonnie Charity, Reginald Sharp (pitcher), Freddie Clark (pitcher), and Preston Simmons. These guys were not professional, most had primary jobs working as farmers. Our rival was a team from Ahoskie, but in my opinion, it wasn't much of a rivalry because the Ahoskie team wasn't very good. There was a team from Newport News, Virginia, I forget the name, but that was a very good team.

The most famous African American I know of to come from the area played major league baseball for the New York Mets, San Francisco Giants, and Cincinnati Reds. He pitched for the Cincinnati Reds in the 1961 World Series. His name was Sherman Jarvis Jones. Sherman was a local boy who we all called Juke. Juke happened to be my wife's, cousin. Juke was a big pitcher at six feet, four inches. Years after retirement, Juke was elected to the Kansas Legislature.

My favorite baseball player of all times was Jackie Robinson, the first African American to play Major League Baseball when he signed with the Brooklyn Dodgers. Jackie endured the worst racism one can imagine, but he endured, as did most of us. He also changed the face of professional sports in America. Today, his uniform number 42 is retired across all major league teams—the only number and player so honored.

A Radio

My family had no formal entertainment in the home until somewhere around 1942 or '43, when we got a radio. We did, however, have a record player a few years prior to obtaining the radio. I purchased most of my records from Columbia Records, a mail order distributor, and purchased from Columbia for years, even after I went into the Army. I have always loved music, and throughout my life, I purchased records, albums, 8-track tapes, cassettes, reel-to-reel, and CDs. I have never purchased music from the Internet, such as iTunes.

I think I was about 16 when we got our first radio, and my favorite show, the one I listened to everyday as soon as I got home from school, was *The Lone Ranger*.

Without electricity, we relied on batteries to generate power for the radio and record player, and those batteries didn't last long. We had to, what I called at the time, rejuvenate, or recharge the batteries, which we did by putting them on the wood heater for a short period of time. We learned that we only had a limited amount of time to heat those batteries, as too much heat would cause them to explode. I'll bet no one uses a heater to recharge batteries today; indeed, everything is thrown away once its run its course. Also, there are rechargeable batteries, where they can be plugged into house current and recharged. After a number of charges, however, these also become throwaways.

T. S. Britt, one of my classmates, came and set up our radio antenna, which allowed us to get different stations. Earlier I indicated that I didn't think that we were more or less well-off than other families, but maybe I was wrong because T. S.'s family owned a radio way before we did, and they also owned an automobile. I don't know what Mr. Britt's occupation was, but they certainly had more material things than most people in the neighborhood. Also, the guy that we rented our house from had a little store out by Pleasant Plains Church, and they had a radio long before we got one. We would go out to his store, hang out, and especially on fight nights listen to the fights (boxing)—me, Bob, Mom, and Dad. Then, when the Britt's got a radio, it was a little closer to where we lived, so we would cut through the woods and go to their house to listen to the fights. They were always gracious and inviting to us. Anyway, I don't know anyone else who had a radio at that time.

Most fights took place at night, so we traveled at night and without light. We certainly didn't mind, as that is simply how we got from place to place. The fighter I most remember from the day was Joe Lewis. For our family listening to the fights on a neighbor's radio was up there with the highest form of entertainment.

Our Pets

What would a boy, or a family for that matter, be in the country without a faithful companion? As a child, we always had at least one dog around the house. The dog I remember most was Billy, which was a really common name for dogs back then. Today, people give their dogs fancy names. For instance, my great-grandchildren have dogs named Jay, Tinker Bell, Luna, and Nala. We also had cats and two pet cows. The dogs were always into something, chasing stuff, even bees. Once, at about the age of seven, I was mimicking the dogs chasing bees and a bee stung my tongue; boy did it hurt. Mama and Grandmamma fixed up some potions that smelled to high heaven; however, the potion made my tongue feel somewhat better. You can bet I never chased bees again.

I also remember an incident where Billy left home for a couple of days and came back with his head swollen three or four times its usual size. We suspected that either he had been bitten by a snake or a gang of bees stung him. Billy was sick for a while, but eventually his head returned to its normal size, and he was okay.

None of the pets we owned lived in the house. The dogs and cats simply slept where it was most comfortable outdoors.

I have always had an affinity for dogs, and my family and I owned at least one dog from my early childhood until my youngest child Sheila became an adult and left home.

The Pleasure of Recreational Intoxicants

For some people, intoxicants are mandatory for their recreational activities. This is not necessarily the case for me, but I did grow up in a time where mood altering drugs—including alcohol, drugs, and tobacco products—were the norm and used by many, many people for enjoyment. I call these intoxicants "vices," and certainly for me and many others, both in my day and today, we depended on these vices.

In the past, it wasn't as readily apparent, but today we know that some of these vices are unhealthy and harmful. Even so, the government finds ways to make money from these unhealthy products, and in the 1940s, '50s, '60s, and '70s, one of the most dangerous vices was given to soldiers. Yes, the military distributed cigarettes to soldiers daily in their C rations. Further, virtually everyone used alcohol products. In the military, most NCOs and officers took lunch breaks where alcohol was consumed.

When I was growing up in Hertford County, the county was dry and remained so until sometime in the 1970s. Being classified as a dry county meant that if someone wanted an alcoholic beverage other than beer, they either had to travel to another county to purchase it; purchase bootleg locally, which was pretty much what everyone did who drank; or make their own spirits. Beer could be legally sold in almost any establishment—bar, café, or grocery store. Wine was probably the alcoholic beverage most consumed, and most of the wine consumed was homemade. Many, many people consumed wine, even children. Take me for one, I began drinking wine at about the age of 10 or 11. My parents made wine, as did I as an adolescent. I mostly made berry wine, where I would go out into the woods, gather a couple of jarfuls of berries, put the berries in a little water in an airtight jug, and let it sit in a dark, cool place. The wine tasted much better when sugar was added to it. The sugar could either be added before the fermenting process began or afterwards. If it was added afterwards, the wine would be resealed and stored for additional fermenting.

My parents and neighbors used various types of fruit for their wines. They always used sugar, and their end product was much superior to mine. Regardless of the taste, someone would drink the wine made.

As I have stated, I believe that most people drink, some more than others. They drank before I was born, and I have no doubt that they will be drinking long after I am gone. My granddad didn't drink heavily, nor did my dad, but they had a "nip" here and there. I never knew either to get intoxicated. They probably didn't get any alcohol from a state store, whereas today most alcohol is sold in state-approved stores where standards can be maintained. Some of the moonshine, white lighting, or what they called bootleg sold back then, as it is today, was dangerous as people would put anything into it when they were brewing it. In North Carolina, the only place to purchase legal liquor products today is through government/state-controlled, Alcohol Beverage Control stores or bars. But for sure there are many folks who prefer the homebrewed stuff.

Another vice that most people I knew used when I was growing up in rural North Carolina was tobacco. My granddad smoked pipes and chewed tobacco, but I can't remember ever seeing him smoke cigarettes. Smoking was primarily the way that men consumed tobacco products back then. My dad also chewed tobacco, but I can't remember him ever smoking anything. Bob, like me, also smoked pipes; but unlike me, I can't recall him ever smoking cigarettes or cigars.

Women typically consumed tobacco products by dipping snuff. Grandma, my mother, and most women I knew dipped snuff. I always thought that the process of dipping snuff was interesting. First off, there was a certain type of tree that was needed for the snuff brush. So to begin the process of making a snuff brush, a branch had to be pulled from a tree. The person who dipped the snuff would then shave the bark off the limb and beat it down to strands that resembled fine brush bristles, like on a tooth brush, and then let it dry out. That was the snuff brush, and when one got ready to dip, they would dip the brush into the snuff tin, wind that brush around in the tin, get about a half teaspoon on it, and put it between the lower lip and gum. Today, I see very few women dipping snuff because it is a nasty addiction that requires constant spitting, and it is just not ladylike, I suppose. It's interesting that to the contrary, today, many men dip snuff.

I guess it is more macho for them to be spitting all over the place.

I dipped snuff for a spell as a child as a medicinal treatment for seizures. I smoked cigarettes for a while, but for most of my adult life, until about the age of 60, I smoked pipes and cigars. I even went as far as experimenting with Marijuana once, somewhere around 1948, but I didn't find it to my liking. Don't tell my grandchildren! I wouldn't want them following my lead on smoking Marijuana, or for that matter, indulging in any of the vices just discussed.

Essie Nora and her cousin Gladys, Juke's mother

My Wife and Life-Long Love, Essie Nora

I didn't meet my wife, Essie Nora Holloman, on the contrary, she met me way back in February 1946, after I got out of the military for the first time. To the best of my recollections, I was walking down Main Street in Ahoskie minding my own business, and this lovely girl with the prettiest smile walked by and stopped to talk to me. I remember as clear as day that she was going to the post office, and she was walking alone. This was one of the rare occasions when she was alone. I was later to find that she had a twin sister and at total of 12 living brothers and sisters, so she was rarely alone. But this girl who stopped to talk with me would later become my bride and wife on May 9, 1947.

Essie Nora lived with her 12 siblings and her mother and father across the railroad tracks, where the colored people lived on a dirt road, Pine Street, in Ahoskie. Shortly after our first meeting, I bumped into Essie Nora again at one of the local cafés in Ahoskie. It wasn't totally coincidental, as Essie Nora had informed me during our first meeting that she liked to dance, and she and her sisters would frequently visit cafés to dance. After bumping into her a couple of times, she allowed me to come to her house for visits.

I was living in Winton about nine miles away and typically came to Ahoskie on Wednesdays, Saturday nights, and Sundays. I would either catch the bus, which always left Ahoskie for Winton and home at about 9 p.m., or I would occasionally ride my bicycle, but riding the bike at night could be dangerous.

Essie Nora's house was always a busy place, with all her siblings, someone was always around. If it wasn't Reva, it was Nellie Gray; if it wasn't Nellie Gray, it was Herbert Glenn; if it wasn't Herbert Glenn, it was Jessie Ray; if it wasn't Jessie Ray, it was William; if it wasn't William, it was Louise, or one of the other siblings, Mary, Martha, Turner Lee, and Walter Raleigh. Of course, Lenora, Essie Nora's twin sister was always, always around. Lenora seemed to always be around, even though Lenora had two or three boyfriends over the course of time that I was dating Essie Nora. Yes, Essie Nora's house was pretty crowded, but I guess I was alright with them because no one ever gave me a problem.

Jessie Ray was my favorite, and he treated me the best. He was the youngest boy, about 14 at the time, while Essie Nora was 19. I really don't know why Jessie Ray treated me so well; after all, he had older brothers to look up to.

Essie Nora's dad rarely said anything to me; neither did her mother, although Tempie was more verbal than her dad. Both of Essie Nora's parents were always polite to me. I had been raised right despite my stubbornness, I was naturally introverted and stayed out of Cal and Tempie's way, so I didn't give them any trouble either. Ms. Tempie worked quite a bit back then, too, she ran a store that was attached to the house but had a separate entrance. In the store she sold treats, cookies, candy, sodas, crackers, pottage meat, etc., and there was a juke box in the store that would play music if you fed it coins, so people would come play music and dance, dance, dance. There was also talk that she sold a taste or two but I can neither confirm nor deny these reports. In addition to the store, I believed that she had another job, as most African American women of the time did. She picked cotton or did some type of farm work.

When Essie Nora and I went on dates, we went to the movies and/or to cafés. I really wasn't a drinker, so at the café we listened to the music, danced, and maybe ate a little. Freeman's café was our number one café, but we also visited Burton's café, Simon's café, and Fleetwood's café.

Herbert Glenn was one of Essie Nora's unique brothers. All of them liked to dance, especially Herbert Glenn, who wasn't a very good dancer, but he liked to get out there on the floor and dance anyway. He danced with girls or by himself. The dance of the time was the jitterbug, and we all liked that high intensity fast paced dancing, including Herbert Glenn, who often jitterbugged alone. You can't imagine what he looked like jitterbugging out there on the dance floor alone.

Essie Nora was also a fine dancer. I wasn't, so she often danced with other boys in the café. When dancing with me, I would miss a step occasionally, and Essie Nora couldn't follow, so we would just have to stop dancing. Some people might say that I danced wild, but that didn't stop me from getting out there on the floor. Maybe Herbert Glenn and I were two peas in a pod when it came to dancing.

Ms. Tempie did have a piccolo, and people would come by and put money in the box and dance, but it wasn't at all like the atmosphere of the cafés. The best dancer in the family was Reva, I believe, and I just loved watching her dance.

After dating for a while, Essie Nora and I got married. It was maybe a year or so after we met. We lived in Winton with my parents after we first got married. Essie Nora stayed there about six months, but she couldn't get along with my mother, so she moved back to Ahoskie with her mom. Henian Senior was the nicest person in the world and could get along with anyone, so he and Essie Nora were best buddies, but her relationship with my mother never materialized.

Essie Nora and I got married in May 1947, and I went back in the Army in March 1948. That was the only way I saw to make peace with my bride and my mother.

*My Bride –
Essie Nora*

Me and Essie Nora

Me and Essie Nora going for a ride

Me and Essie Nora in retirement

Essie Nora's mother, Ms. Tempie – in front of her shop

Drafted into the US Army

In the spring of 1942, I received my initial draft notice indicating that Uncle Sam wanted me, but since I was only 17 years old, I received a deferment until I turned 18 in December 1942. I formally registered for the draft in January 1943, after I turned 18. I suppose that since I was a senior in high school, I was allowed to continue in school until graduation. They also drafted some of my schoolmates out of high school, and I think that most of them entered the Army before graduating.

Bob was also drafted into the US Army. He was drafted a few months before me, in March, while I was drafted in June. After BCT and AIT, Bob would go to war in Europe, while I would go to war in the Pacific Theater. Both of my mother's children were in war zones at the same time. Although there were only a few months' difference between our Army entry times, Bob would hit the war much sooner than I, as his truck driving school was much shorter than the school to which I was assigned.

On June 14, 1943, I became a soldier at Fort Bragg, North Carolina My induction center, Fort Bragg, "the Home of the

Screaming Eagles," was the central induction center for the state of North Carolina. Fort Bragg would also be the place where my eldest son and namesake Edward would be assigned to permanent party after he entered the Army and completed Airborne training. My initial enlistment lasted two years, eight months, and ten days.

I had no problems with entering the Army. You see, I was a simple country boy who had wanted to get away from home and see the world, and certainly I would get that opportunity. In the next six years, I would travel to Texas, New Jersey, California, Hawaii, Australia, India, Saipan, and Korea. I traveled halfway around the world. In the 21 years I was in the Army, I would be a 90-millimeter gun commander, radar operator, radio operator, radar repairman, nuclear weapons technician, and a supply sergeant. Getting drafted or entering the Army was actually my second option for leaving home. My first option was the Civilian Conservation Corps, but my mom shot that out of the sky.

Reporting for the draft meant that I reported to the Draft Board and was given a physical, which of course I passed. After the physical, I was asked which branch of the military I wanted. There were only two available for most African Americans to choose from at the time: the Army or the Navy. The Air Force had not yet been formed. On the other hand, the Marine Corps, which had been around since at least 1775, was pretty much off-limits to African Americans back then and was the last branch to accept "blacks" or "coloreds."

I wanted nothing to do with the Navy. I didn't want to be on the ocean with all of that water, so I chose the Army but was surprised to learn that the choice might not be up to me. My recruiter informed me that everyone was selecting the Army. He didn't know why and didn't care. They needed more people for the Navy, so I would have to wait. The recruiter told me that I might have to be drafted into the Navy and advised me to take a seat and wait to see what branch of the military I would be assigned to. I learned a lesson that day—a lesson I would carry with me for the next 21 years: how to "hurry up and wait." That hour or so that I waited was one of the most anxious waits of my life, but in the end, everything worked out, as they got enough recruits for the Navy and I was Army bound. I could breathe again.

I was soon enlisted in the United States Army and would be Army Strong the remainder of my life. I was a "buck private," Enlisted-one, or E-1, the lowest ranking individual in the Army. As I was preparing to depart the reception center, the recruiter advised me that I was "in the wrong line, stupid. You need to get in the line with your proper race, the white folk line." Of course, I told him I was black, and I was in the right line, so for the remainder of that enlistment, I served in all-black units, except for senior officers.

Many of the fair skinned African Americans of that time passed as white. I remember fair skinned African Americans moving from Ahoskie to Portsmouth or Norfolk, Virginia and getting jobs at the shipyard. They passed for white simply because certain government shipyard jobs were off-limits to blacks. These individuals performed just as well in their positions as the whites did, but for me I was black and proud of it.

At Fort Bragg and at the induction center before I even made it to Basic Combat Training, I got into the only fight I was in during my 21 years in the military. I don't even know what started the fight. I guess it was my first time away from home, and I just had to prove myself. For sure it wasn't much of a fight. I remember getting punched good in the jaw and landing a couple of punches to my opponents' stomach, which was always my fighting style. Go for the gut, knock the wind out of your opponent, and you could control him. I must have learned this style standing outside of the local store on fight night listening to a *Friday Night Fight*. A lieutenant, of all people, saw us fighting, broke it up, and that was that. That was the last fight I was ever in; however, I came close to getting in a fight with a white boy at Fort Monmouth, which I will talk about later.

Basic Combat Training

After induction, I was transported by train to Texas for Basic Combat Training (BCT). This was to a place named Camp Wallace, located in Galveston on the Gulf of Mexico about 50 miles or so east of Houston. Recruits were transported on a regular passenger train, and the ride was hot as the dickens, as there was no air conditioning back then. But that ride would be seen as a first-class ride compared to a train ride across India that I would take the next year.

BCT for us was to be in the dead of summer in the sweltering heat; it was hot, dusty, and just nasty. We were in Texas during the hurricane season, and being on the Gulf made it quite humid most of the time. We had to endure one hurricane while we were there, but it didn't stop us from training, except for the actual day when the hurricane hit land. Everyone had to stay in the barracks that day.

The barracks was a two-story building, and on the day that the hurricane hit land, soldiers housed on the first floor were moved upstairs to the second floor where I was bunked. Water covered the ground and came up to the top of the barracks' steps, but it didn't breach the doorway.

BCT started sometime in July, and I believe it lasted about 12 to 16 weeks. As an E-1, I got paid $50.00 a month, and they automatically deducted $4.00 to take care of our laundry bill. After taxes, the rest was ours. We got paid in cash on the first of the month in a big gymnasium.

Recruits were between the ages of 18 and 45 and had varying interests, but card playing on payday was a mainstay, except for me. There were some card sharks who were not beyond cheating, and on a regular basis I saw individuals lose their entire paycheck gambling in a couple of hours on payday. I didn't gamble but never seemed to have any money left at the end of the month. Maybe it was because I didn't have a bank account or simply wasn't used to having any money and didn't know how to budget.

About a month or so into BCT, I began buying US Saving Bonds for $18.00 a month, and that didn't leave a whole lot of money left, but I was able to save a little bit. After my tour, I had planned to buy a motorcycle and had enough money, but my brother Bob talked me out of it, suggesting that we buy a car together. Well, Bob moved to Norfolk, Virginia and got married, and I never bought that car nor the motorcycle. I ended up just blowing my savings. I guess it was a good thing that I didn't buy a motorcycle because when I was home on leave, somewhere around 1955, I completely rolled my Studebaker, the first car I owned, in one of my former teacher's yard. I didn't get a scratch. If, on the other hand, I had been on a motorcycle, most likely I would have killed myself because I liked speed. My son Douglas owned motorcycles and did okay, so maybe I would have also, but I will never know because I didn't buy one.

In the 1940s, Basic Training consisted of two parts: Basic Combat Training (BCT) and Advanced Individual Training (AIT). My basic training was held at Camp Wallace and later, the second part of basic training, AIT, was held at Camp Davis Army Airfield. The group of men with whom I entered BCT would be together for the next three years, and we would all go to World War II together.

BCT is the program of physical and mental training required in order for civilians to become United States Army Soldiers, the best soldiers in the world. At that time, BCT was carried out at several Army posts across the United States. BCT was and is designed to be highly intense and challenging, to make boys into fighting men and to weed out the weak. I say boys, but again the age range for recruits at that time was between 18 and 45.

The training challenges come as much from the difficulty of physical exercise as it does from the emotional and psychological demands placed on the recruits. This is where new enlistees learn about the fundamentals of being a soldier—from combat techniques to the proper way to address a superior; how to fold clothes and make a bed; how to clean, load, and fire weapons; how to clean toilets and re-clean toilets; and for some good hygiene practices. BCT is where new enlistees undergo the rigorous training to prepare their bodies and their minds for the eventual physical and mental strain of combat/war.

A key or fundamental component to the physical training is running, "double time" everywhere, and I mean double timing everywhere one goes. Oh, and then there are pushups, pushups, and more pushups, even pushups in your dreams. I imagine that my biceps doubled in size during basic training because of all the pushups I did.

One of the most difficult and essential lessons learned in BCT training is self-discipline, as it introduces the new recruit/soldiers to a strict daily schedule that entails many duties and high expectations, for which most civilians are not immediately prepared. The typical day begins at maybe four thirty in the morning and lasts until about eight or nine at night—and frequently later. And that 4:30 a.m. start time might include crawling under the barracks in the dark just for the sake of it.

All soldiers in BCT are required to attend some sort of class throughout the day. One of the most important classes was that of the use of weapons—their personal weapon, not a gun. We couldn't dare call our weapon a gun. At minimum, that behavior would result in a temper tantrum by one of our black drill instructors/sergeants, with him screaming as if the world were coming to an end. He would then make the offending soldier and everyone around him push the ground, or what is more commonly termed pushups.

The weapon of choice in the US Army at that time was the M1 Garand, a 30-caliber semi-automatic rifle that holds an eight-round magazine clip. We learned to fire the M1 from a standing position, kneeling position, and from the prone position; we fired this weapon day and night until we qualified and then some. We also received classes in hand grenade throwing, firing anti-tank missile launchers, and mortars.

Weaponry was not the only essential for graduating from basic training. We had to learn the Army Core Values, how to march in formation, battlefield maneuvering, and first aid.

Drill sergeants or drill instructors (DIs) were our teachers and were responsible for most of the training we received in BCT. The DIs were with us constantly. It seemed as if they were there 24/7—all the time, and I mean all the time, throughout the training process, instructing, and correcting. I can assure you that these individuals were not mild mannered and nothing like anyone's high school teacher or parent. They barked, screamed, yelled, and intimidated us at every turn, whether we were doing things right or wrong.

Back in those days, they slapped, punched, and kicked trainees until the trainee got it right. They were responsible for ensuring that we learned but also for our safety, for instance ensuring that we didn't blow ourselves to smithereens during grenade training, or that we didn't shoot ourselves or someone else when on the firing range. I can hear them now. "Didn't I tell you to keep that weapon pointed down range!"

DIs were like they have always been—loud, intimidating, and yelling every command. But they didn't intimidate me. One day, my platoon sergeant was yelling at me for something, I don't remember what, and I told him, "You don't have to yell at me, I ain't no dog." I guess I was supposed to get chewed out for that comment, but I didn't, and from then on, he talked to me in a civil manner, like I was a person. I guess he thought I was a softie or something and couldn't stand to get yelled at. I wasn't nasty; I was just assertive. You don't have to talk to me like a dog. I grew up in the country, and so I was probably pretty naive. In the country, outside of school, you were pretty isolated, not exposed to much at all. We couldn't learn from TV or radio because TV didn't exist, and it was a while before we owned a radio. Dick Tracy was the only one back then who had computers and cell phones, and he was a comic strip hero.

Basic training is a mind game, but it didn't affect me that much. It did seem to affect those guys from New York, who didn't want to take orders and who were constantly being corrected. In BCT, I would befriend a guy by the name of Lawson. He was from the city, so he was a little more sophisticated than I was. I was fortunate that he was my friend.

As mentioned, we trained all day from before sunup until well after the sun went down; but also, every night, at least two recruits from the platoon (the 30 or so individuals in our barracks) were responsible for patrolling the barracks' area, watching for fires, watching for recruits attempting to leave the barracks' area, going AWOL, etc. The people standing watch did not get "compensatory time off the next day." Recruit pairs worked two-hour shifts, one group relieving another. Later, in war zones, there would also be groups of soldiers up all night—one group relieving another to guard against attacks while the rest of the platoon slept or rested. In basic training, these patrols are generally referred to as fire guard/watch.

In addition to learning basic combat skills, my unit also learned the fundamentals of the 90-millimeter anti-aircraft gun. These guns were not personal weapons, and they were called guns. They were ground based and fired a shell that was about two feet long, three inches in diameter, and weighed approximately 21 pounds.

Soon after I arrived to BCT, I was privileged to be promoted to Enlisted-2 (E2) the second lowest ranking individual in the Army—still a private. With this promotion, I became a gun commander, the supervisor of a team of ten or so recruits responsible for preparing, maintaining, and firing that big, loud, 90-millimeter anti-aircraft gun.

As a gun commander, I gave all the orders to fire the gun. They chose people for certain occupations in the Army by their score on the Army General Classification Test (AGCT). I scored high and had a high school diploma, so I suppose that is why I was promoted to gun commander. Being a high school graduate was unique at the time. Very few of the individuals with whom I was in BCT were graduates.

I could not imagine, only several weeks prior, that I would be supervising men 15 to 20 years my senior. I was a boy, and they were grown men. I was just a shy, introverted country boy who had difficulty looking the sergeant in the eye, let alone screaming and shouting orders in the chaos of firing that huge gun.

Early on in this assignment, I simply gave orders, and one of my soldiers shouted out the order so everyone understood, but it didn't take me long to shoulder the full responsibilities of leading this team of soldiers. As the gun commander, I didn't have to stand on the gun. I stood back and gave the commands.

Socialization and interacting with different cultures is probably one of those unwritten expectations for BCT. Although we were all African Americans, we were from different cultures. Some of us were from farms, some from the cities, from the north, from the south, some educated, others not so well educated, some from large families, and some from small ones.

In BCT, I made a couple of new friends. My best buddy, from the time we arrived to Camp Davis until the time we were discharged in 1946, was a guy by the name of Nariah Lawson. Lawson was from Kinston, North Carolina. Our bunks in basic were right next to each other. The DIs would come through looking for someone for detail, and if he saw one of us, he called us by one name Newsome/Lawson. He didn't care which one it was; he simply would call Newsome/Lawson. I guess we might have even looked a little bit alike. We were maybe the same complexion, same build, maybe I was a little taller, and of course we both spoke in the same southern drawl. When Newsome/Lawson was called, we typically both responded, and I don't really think it mattered who responded. The military really encourages partnerships, and they even have a name for this relationship. For the Army, it's "battle buddy." For the Air Force, its "wingman." This special relationship, or partnership, between service members provides companionship, support, and encouragement to each other and facilitates problem-solving.

Another one of my closest friends, battle buddies, from BCT was a fellow by the name of Wansley. Charles Wansley was originally from Louisiana, but he eventually landed in New York after he got out of the Army. For a long time after we got out of the Army, not only did Charles write me but we were such close friends he also wrote my mother on a regular basis. We didn't have access to telephones, so soldiers kept in contact with family and friends by writing. Can you imagine actually writing letters—not texting or emailing, but writing?

During the 20 years I was in the Army, not one of my schoolmates wrote to me, although I wrote them—especially some of the girls. I was surprised no one wrote back. My mama wrote me maybe a couple of times a month. Dad didn't write as much, but he wrote regularly. On the other hand, I would write him a couple times weekly. Andrew and I also wrote regularly.

Eating in the mess hall was a place where there was a social pecking order, and I learned about that order. When we got to BCT in Texas, we ate family style, where we were marched to the mess hall, selected a table to sit at, and the cooks would put the food on the table. Well, we had some Yankee boys from New York who were real food hounds. As soon as the food went on the table, the bowls were grabbed and shared only with the other New York recruits, and it would only touch the table again when the bowl was empty, before the rest of us got anything to eat. So, we would have to go back up to the serving line to get something. Rarely did we get anything off the table. Me and Lawson were buddies through and through, and we had to go up to the line almost daily to get breakfast, lunch, and dinner.

In the Army and in BCT, there was the expectation that we were our brother's keepers, despite the selfishness of the New York boys. A couple of guys were kinda slow and were always messing up—in formation, on the firing line, or wherever. We did all we could to bring them along, but the DIs had lots of ways to motivate them. One of the ways for getting their attention was to require them to go out in the field and dig a six-foot hole, or go under the barracks and dig a hole. As mentioned, others would slap, punch, or kick the poor performing soldier.

Socialization and team building also occurred during formal formation movements, either marching or running. The DIs and eventually the recruits learned cadences or stories that were sung. Some examples of the cadences sung might go as follows:

Ain't no use in going home/Jody's got your girl and gone. Ain't no use in feelin' blue/Jody's got your sister, too. Ain't no use in lookin' back/Jody's got your Cadillac..."

or

Hi Ho Diddly Bop/I wish I was back on the block/ With my rifle in my hand/I wanna be a fighting man. Hi Ho Diddly Bop/I wish I was back on the block/ With my woman in my arms/I wanna be a lovin' man Hi Ho Diddly Bop/I wish I was back on the block/With my bottle in my hand/I wanna be a drinking man.

or

Here we go again/Same old stuff again/Marching down the avenue/Few more days and we'll be though/I won't have to look at you/So, I'll be glad and so will you.

BCT tamed most of us. I mean, there were some really wild guys who arrived to basic from New York, Chicago, and the far reaches of North Carolina. There was one guy who was more of a challenge than most, and he was a gun commander, like myself. I remember this guy was from somewhere around Durham, North Carolina, and he had studied karate and taught it to us. I am not sure how gifted he was or what belt ranking this guy was, but he knew more karate than any of us, and so this made him an expert.

The karate knowledge he had certainly didn't translate into serenity or tranquility, as this guy had a temper. He was a real hot head. Indeed, he got busted or reduced in rank for getting into a fight with someone else from our platoon, but he graduated BCT with the rest of us and moved on to AIT.

Advanced Individual Training

Upon graduating from Basic Combat Training, my entire unit traveled from Texas to North Carolina for Advanced Individual Training (AIT). As mentioned, back in those days cohorts of entire units entered the military and served their entire tour, usually three years, together. Today it is my understanding that it is extremely rare for the most basic BCT unit, a platoon of 30 people, to have more than two or three to be assigned to the same AIT unit after graduating from BCT. Typically, there are maybe four platoons in a BCT battery, so there are hundreds of individuals being trained. But again, there are a very limited number of soldiers having consecutive assignments from BCT, to AIT, to permanent party.

Although the unit moved in unison, there were stragglers. At Camp Davis, a new African American officer was assigned to our unit, a home boy named Lt. Cherry. Lt. Cherry was from Ahoskie, North Carolina, or more specifically Bertie County You see, in my neck of the woods, Ahoskie is a hub or central city, and Bertie County shared a border with Hertford County, where the city of Ahoskie is located. Ahoskie is one of the largest cities in the area, so for us Bertie County is a suburban community of Ahoskie.

I don't know what city in Bertie County Lt. Cherry was from, but he was a homeboy. Not only that, Lt. Cherry was an officer, and I was more than proud to salute him. There was no one in the military more respected by the troops than an African American Officer.

Lt. Cherry, like myself, got out of the Army after the war, and we met again as civilians when I was dating the woman who became my life long partner and wife. I introduced him to Essie Nora at a dance at the Elks Home in Ahoskie. The Elks Home was the meeting place in Ahoskie for "The Benevolent and Protective Order of Elks." Some people describe Elks as an organization similar to the Shriners or Masons. Anyway, the Elks is a fraternity with an emphasis on benevolence and charity. I became an Elk member in Enterprise, Alabama in 1953. In addition to meetings, the Elks Home was a gathering place for parties, which my wife and I attended on a fairly regular basis.

Essie Nora didn't know Lt. Cherry, but he had taught her twin sister, Lenora, at the Robert L. Vann High School before the war. You might ask why he taught Essie Nora's twin sister and not her. Well, Lenora had broken her leg in junior high school and had to be out of school for a while, so she was a grade behind Essie Nora.

Between BCT and AIT, I was given a three-day furlough/pass, and you can bet I headed for home. It was a delight to see my parents and friends again after being away from home for the first time in my life; however, over the next twenty or so years, I spent very little time in North Carolina, let alone Winton. Rather, I would travel the world. Certainly, I did not spend another Christmas with my mother, father, or brother for the 21-year period I was in the Army. Of course, I took leave periodically, but it was expensive for our family of four children to take regular vacations and return home. Fortunately, or you might say unfortunately, in the Army, a soldiers' duty station changes at least every three years—sometime less frequently and rarely more. Some of my duty stations were "unaccompanied, hardship tours," where I couldn't take the family. On these assignments, the family would go back home to North Carolina and stay there until I returned. So, during the 21 years I was in the military, I had maybe 21 assignments, to include three hardship tours. All of the hardship tours were to Korea.

AIT is where recruits are trained in their various Army career paths, or Military Occupational Specialty (MOS). Camp Davis is where we had AIT training. It was located maybe 20 miles south of Wilmington, North Carolina, a little more than 100 miles from home in Winton. It was on what is called the outer banks of North Carolina and was a little less than 100 miles north of Myrtle Beach, South Carolina. Camp Davis was within walking distance of the US Marine Corp Base, Camp Lejeune, at most 25 miles away. And the little city outside the gate only had about six stores, but these stores must have gotten rich off of us.

At AIT, the exclusive focus of our training was on the 90-millimeter anti-aircraft gun as we prepared to go to war. The location of our training unit was important, as we fired those big guns towards the ocean. You see, there were times when the shells did not explode the way they were supposed to. There were other times when we didn't get our aim exactly right. This could cause serious problems, so firing them toward the ocean helped avoid civilian casualties.

We had been given a good introduction to the 90-millimeter gun in BCT, but now the real training would begin. However, my assignment changed when we got to Camp Davis. Upon our arrival, I was informed that I had yet again been volunteered for a different job. I was informed that I would become a radar operator. Another guy from my BCT platoon was also volunteered to become a radar operator. He was Sgt. J. T. Miller, the only person I knew in my basic training unit who had some college education. I guess that is why he was promoted to sergeant and volunteered to work as a radar operator. I imagine that he was also probably pretty smart. Anyway, he was a sergeant and outranked me by one rank, as I was now an E-3, Private First Class.

I suspect that my aptitude in math contributed to my being selected to be trained as a radar operator. Radar operator training was not as formal as you might expect. It primarily consisted of on-the-job training (OJT), and I don't know who taught the people who taught us—but the guy in charge of training was a Section Chief E-5 Sgt. Binus Parks.

You might ask, why is it important to have radar operators in a 90-millimeter anti-air craft gun unit? Well, there are multiple moving parts to targeting airplanes and then shooting them out of the sky. A fundamental component in locating the planes that need to be shot down is the job of the radar operator. The work of identifying and targeting enemy planes requires radar detection interfaced with a computer.

The computer and radar were located in vans set apart from the guns. Radar/computer operators worked in teams of two, and our offices were fairly comfortable. They were outfitted with mobile office chairs, something few people in the field had, and consoles where the computer radars were located. Each individual in a pair was responsible for monitoring an oscilloscope (scope for short). The scope was made into a cabinet, one focusing on the trajectory azimuth and the other on elevation. There was a crank at our work station, and this allowed us to manually adjust the antenna, tracking the enemy air plane; however, the antenna could also be controlled automatically. We primarily used the automatic controls.

The antenna would send data or a signal through a computer to a control box and then to the guns via long, thick cables. The computer computed the speed of the airplane based upon information received from the radar. The coordinates of the enemy plane would be communicated to the gun team; the gun commander, the loader, the two individuals on the gun setting the gun's azimuth and elevation (trackers), fuse setter, and two handlers (primarily responsible for making sure ammunition was available). At this point, the gun was ready to be fired.

As part of the unit, or battery, there were cooks, medics, truck drivers, mechanics, people who ordered ammunition and other supplies, people who operated the gun, people who repaired the gun, people who operated the radar, as well as people who repaired the radar. And what would antiaircraft gun training be without the opportunity to shoot aircraft out of the sky? So, there were also pilots who worked with our units. These pilots pulled drones, released them, and flew away. This allowed us to fire at the drone and not shoot the plane, which we almost did on a couple of occasions.

By the time I graduated from AIT, I guess you could say that I was kind of an expert on that gun. I knew everything to know about the gun and how the radar and computer integrated into tracking and killing enemy aircraft.

At the conclusion of AIT, I was given a ten-day pass and again returned home, but it was a short trip, as those ten days flew by. I wish I could have stayed longer, as our unit was scheduled to be transferred to India and the war theater. Certainly, I was lucky, as I only had a relatively short trip home. Others in my outfit had much longer distances to travel before they arrived home.

Once back at Camp Davis from leave, we immediately began our plans for deployment to India, but we would have several stops at various staging areas before we departed the US.

March to War

On our march to war through India to Saipan, we deployed from Camp Davis through Fort Bragg to Camp Beauregard and Camp Livingston in Louisiana. These two camps were neighboring camps. The largest was Camp Beauregard, but both camps were geographically connected, and we trained in both. We were transported to Camp Beauregard via train, and our guns and other equipment were transported by another train. In many instances, soldiers and equipment, to include heavy guns, would move in convoys. I don't know why we didn't move that way.

Camp Beauregard in the 1940s was a major WWII training area. It is estimated that a half million soldiers or more participated in war games held in Camp Beauregard and surrounding camps prior to deploring to the war. Camp Beauregard was located in the Deep South, where the climate was hot and humid, making it an ideal climate for training American troops preparing for war in East Asia.

We trained at Camp Beauregard for a couple of months before heading to California, where we boarded ships, India bound. The trip from Louisiana to California was in the summer of 1943, and we traveled by train, not airplane, which is the primary mode of transportation for the military today.

California was just a debarkation station, as we did no training in California. The cruise to India lasted 32 days, and it was not a luxury cruise. We traveled aboard a troop-carrying ship, the *George M. Randal*. There were at least 500 soldiers on the ship, as our battalion alone was composed of Alpha, Bravo, Charlie, Delta, and Headquarters Batteries. The African American soldiers' berthing quarters were on the very bottom of the ship. If one of those German U-boat torpedoes were to have hit our ship, the African American soldiers would have been the first to perish, while it would have been plausible for others to survive.

Our quarters were extremely cramped, and we slept in bunks stacked three high. The air in the bottom of the ship was often stale and musty, as people smoked cigarettes and cigars—a real cancer chamber. A saving grace was that we were allowed the luxury of coming up to the deck of the ship once daily. We cherished the opportunity to get to the deck. The expectation was that we would get some exercise, which we did, but we also got some leisure time on deck and fresh air. On the trip over, we had one soldier who had an emotional/mental meltdown. Forgive me, but he just went nuts, and by the time we arrived to India, he had to be transferred out of the war theater and back home.

On our way to India, we ported at Hobart Island in Tasmania, Australia for four days, and I went ashore for one day of leave. From Australia, we traveled to Bombay, India and then by rail to the province of Assam, India in the northern part of India, which was about a three-day train trip. That rail trip was something, as the train didn't have seats, it had wooden planks that we sat on or slept on. For most of us, it was more comfortable for us to lay or sit on our duffle bags—bags that contained all of our possessions, primarily military clothing. From Assam, we traveled to Calcutta, where we stayed for approximately one month, and then took a 12-day boat trip to Saipan and the Marianas. Again, our berthing area on the trip was the bottom of the ship.

When I was in India, I got my only care package from home, but it was so far away and the shipping was so slow, and there were no preservatives used at the time, so by the time my package arrived, the food had spoiled and was not edible.

In India, I visited the Burning Ghats on the Ganges River. The Burning Ghats was/is an outdoor crematory. Cremation is one of the rites of passage in the Hindu tradition—a major Indian Religion. The Ghats are dedicated to this cremation ritual. The ceremony I witnessed had these piles of wood that were lit, and I believe there were four elaborately dressed corpses, which were placed on separate piles of burning wood. At the time of the cremation, or "last rites," a prayer was performed. The Ghats fires have reportedly been burning for thousands of years. Hindus believe that the worn-out body must first be burned in order to liberate the soul. The person's ashes must then be scattered so that the soul can achieve nirvana.

In India, as we walked through the crowded streets, we also saw cobra snake charmers. These guys would play this little flute and a cobra would rise out of a basket. To this day, I believe that the cobras had been defanged. I just don't believe they would take that risk of being that close to such a dangerous snake. I guess you might call me a skeptic.

In the Marianas, we bivouacked and built relatively permanent quarters in Saipan, where we would live and train for the next year or more. In Saipan, our unit typically attended lectures, trained on the 90 mm anti-aircraft gun, participated in calisthenics, and organized athletics. We also went out on patrols, and on one of our patrols, we captured a couple of Japanese soldiers—three males and one female. I am not sure whether we actually captured them or if they surrendered. Fortunately for me, my unit never participated in actual combat operations (except for patrols on Saipan), nor were we close enough to battle to even hear a gun shot. We were, however, awarded battle stars for being in the war zone. I would also be awarded a battle star for my first tour in Korea.

I was in the Marianas when the Enola Gay left Tinian for its mission of dropping the nuclear bombs on Hiroshima and Nagasaki. The island of Tinian was within eyesight of the island upon which we were stationed. As a matter of fact, one day we witnessed a US Army Air Corps plane taking off from Tinian headed our way, and immediately one of the engines caught fire. The plane started going down, but no one parachuted out. The plane seemed to make a smooth landing in the ocean à la Chesley Sullenberger, a former military pilot who, as a civilian passenger pilot, landed a plane loaded with passengers safely on the Hudson River in 2009.

In Saipan, we had a fair amount of free time, and I spent time swimming and cliff diving. Imagine, here I am, a boy from the country used to swimming in creeks and rivers.

There certainly were no pools that existed in Winton in those days for African Americans.

We would also go to the outdoor theater and watch movies. Intramural boxing on base was also an activity that we enjoyed. We happened to have Mathew Jackson—we called him Stonewall Jackson, the sixth army middleweight champion in our unit. Stonewall was not only a boxer but also a trainer for the unit boxers. He boxed in the Army, was an amateur champion, and also boxed as a pro. There were quite a few amateur and pro fighters in the military at the time. Jimmy Braddock, who was later to fight Joe Lewis, the Brown Bomber, was also in the Army at that time. As a matter of fact, Joe Lewis was actually the heavyweight champion of the world when he enlisted. No, he was not drafted into the Army, he enlisted. He enlisted in 1942 and was discharged in 1945. Despite his popularity, he was exposed to untold racism, as were all African Americans of the time. I would have given anything to see the Brown Bomber fight at the height of his career.

Our Officers

Before I make this limited discussion about the officers I encountered during my first tour of duty in the Army, I feel as if it is important to preface my comments with a statement about discrimination. You see, although I had only been in the military for maybe six months, during this period, I learned more about discrimination than I had my entire life in rural North Carolina.

The African American officers in our unit were all junior grade officers, first and second lieutenants. The senior officers in our unit, and most other African American units, were all white. Senior officers were battery or battalion commanders of the rank of captain, major, or higher.

When I enlisted in the Army, it was the policy of the Army to give command of black troops to white southern officers because, I suppose, they theorized that white southerners knew how to "hound/ride/harass black soldiers." You see, it was a commonly held belief by many whites, probably most if not all, that African Americans were lazy, shiftless, and unintelligent. Whites, educated or not, to include the officer corps did not trust black folk to supervise black folk.

Only white people with a plantation owners' mentality could get a good day's work out of a black person.

I can remember that the two most nasty, racist people I have met in my 90 years on this earth were senior company grade or junior field grade officers. In our unit, Charlie Battery 234 Artillery, during basic training there was this battalion commander, a lieutenant colonel, and his executive officer, a major—both white officers who I won't dignify by giving their names—who were loathed by the enlisted African American soldiers. One element of their jobs was to inspect the troops on a regular basis—and we got inspected weekly. Our battalion commander was so nasty that when he inspected us, some of my colleagues would be so frightened and get so nervous that they just couldn't function; they would freeze. They couldn't execute what was called inspection arms or even manage the most basic solute, and this gave the lieutenant colonel fodder to ridicule those soldiers and all the other African American soldiers in ear shot. A weapons inspection was always part of the inspection, and many of my fellow enlisted couldn't get their weapons up into inspection positions, something they had done a thousand times.

My dignity, esteem, or just plain old stubbornness (remember how I wouldn't cry when Mom whipped me) would not allow me to show any fear in his presence. I might have been a little more emboldened or arrogant around him, in fact. I had come into my own in only a couple of months as a soldier. Maybe I did learn something from those young black lieutenants, but for sure I hated him. I believe we all hated him, but I forced myself to be strong around him. Every time I saw him, I would curse him in my mind, thinking of him as an inferior, and look him directly in the eye without flinching. He could say what he wanted, but I would not allow him to make me nervous or embarrass me. I guess that some of my hatred stemmed from that old white farmer who stole eggs, vegetables, and fruit from my grandparents.

I remember one particular incident when we were having rifle practice on the range, and one of our junior African American officers, a Lt. Jones from New York, was in charge. Lt. Jones was a young African American rebel who took nothing off of anyone, especially white folk, period, enlisted or officer, regardless of rank. One day, we were going on a march through a predominately white section of the camp, and a white sergeant failed to salute him. Many white enlisted on camp would demonstrate their disrespect for the black officers by refusing to salute them. Well, Lt. Jones was having none of it. He stopped our marching formation immediately and blessed/cursed the sergeant out, forcing him to go get his company commander immediately to discuss his indiscretion. I am sure that nothing came of it because all blacks were viewed as second class citizens in society and in the Army of 1943. We were grateful that Lt. Jones stood his ground. He was our man.

The next incident I remember regarding our Lt. Jones occurred when we were on the firing range, where we qualified with our weapons/rifles. Well, this white executive officer, a major, came by, and as he usually did, he attempted to find something wrong with whomever or whatever. On this particular occasion, he told Lt. Jones to look at one of his soldiers lying prone in one of the most basic firing positions, suggesting that the firing position was incorrect. The major informed Lt. Jones that the soldier didn't know what he is doing and directed Lt. Jones to get down on the ground and show the soldier how to fire his weapon. Lt. Jones looked at the major indignantly and said, "That's not my job. I have sergeants who are responsible for teaching soldiers appropriate firing position," I'm not getting down anywhere. No, Lt. Jones didn't take any stuff from any of those white folk, and we loved and respected him.

Our lieutenant colonel was eventually transferred out of our unit. I am not aware of the reason for his transfer. We did see him once while we were marching in formation to an exercise and noticed that he had been reduced in rank to major. Life catches up with us, doesn't it?

There was another incident involving one of our lieutenants. I can't remember his name, but on this particular day, the major who was the executive officer was inspecting the mess hall (where we ate), and the supply and arms room, where all of the weapons were stored—including M1s and .45-caliber pistols. The old major had taken a seat and was talking to the lieutenant in the arms room. The major grabbed a rifle and held it up, looking up the barrel, and said, "This rifle is filthy." The lieutenant immediately snatched the rifle out of his hands, looked up the barrel himself, and stated, "I don't see nothing wrong with it. It's fine. Let's move on."

In addition to the lieutenant colonel and major, there was another purely rotten officer. I don't remember his rank, but he would just ride us day in and day out for no reason. No one liked this officer, as he was especially nasty to us and one of the officers who happened to be Jewish. So, during the last bivouac of BCT, which lasted two weeks, we plotted to assault this officer late at night. Somehow, someone found out about the planned assault and foiled it. I guess you might call this a mutiny if we were in the Navy. Certainly, in Vietnam, this type of behavior, "fragging," occurred periodically for poorly performing, typically a junior officer, as they slept. I suppose we were all supposed to get court marshaled for this incident, and I have no inclination as to why we didn't.

All of the African American soldiers were proud of the black officers. All of these officers had backbones and would stand up to any of the white officers on our behalf. I suspect that they received good training at the Reserve Officer Training Corp (ROTC) or the Officer's Candidate School (OCS). Certainly, I don't think too many of our officers graduated from the US service academies, although at the time there was one African American graduate from West Point, the US Army Service Academy. His name was Benjamin Oliver Davis Jr., and he graduated in 1936.

By the time I entered the military, Benjamin Davis was a Lieutenant Colonel in the Army Air Core and was flying missions as a Tuskegee Airman. I imagine that Lt. Jones had the backbone of Benjamin Davis, who endured four years at West Point as the only African American Cadet there, where all of his white classmates refused to talk to him—"the silent treatment"—for the four years he was at the academy. Years later, not only would West Point welcome African Americans but it would also welcome women. Indeed, my grandson Henian would marry a young woman, Domeca, who graduated from West Point.

Getting back to Lt. Jones, he interacted with us as if he were just an average guy. He was a little older than I was, maybe in his mid- to late twenties, but he was a real soldier, much more than I could aspire to.

There was another incident involving one of our lieutenants. I can't remember his name, but on this particular day, the major, executive officer, was inspecting the mess hall (where we ate), and the supply and arms room, where all of the weapons were stored—including M1s and 45-caliber pistols. The old major had taken a seat and was talking to the lieutenant in the arms room. The major grabbed a rifle and held it up, looking up the barrel, and said, "This rifle is filthy." The lieutenant immediately snatched the rifle out of his hands, looked up the barrel himself, and stated, "I don't see nothing wrong with it. It's fine. Let's move on."

I am not sure why the white superior officers didn't challenge these lieutenants, but for the most part, they didn't push back—at least in my presence. Seventy years later, I still admired those guys. Absolutely we need more people like that today—people who will stand up for right and against bullies, despite the potential negative consequences. I would describe these two officers, and later Lt. Colonel Chase, and even later General Colin Powell, as hard working, intelligent, strong willed, determined, and fearless. These are absolutely characteristics of the finest soldiers in the world. These characteristics were the exact opposite of what the white gentry of 1944 thought about African Americans.

Although those officers were bold and challenging and admired, their style never rubbed off on me, as I tended to be a little more easygoing and really never had a hard time with any of those white officers. But again, I had a very light complexion and could have passed for white, so I may have been spared some of the abuse that most African American enlisted soldiers endured. Certainly, throughout American history, fair-skinned African Americans have been preferred. The fair-skinned African American was allowed to work in the big house away from the elements such as the heat of summer and cold of winter, while the not-so-preferred darker skinned field negro endured much, much harsher treatment and even severe abuse. I was fair-skinned, my brother, who was brown skinned only a little darker than I, and who I perceived to be more intelligent and wiser, didn't seem to get the same opportunities I did while in the Army. I am just speculating, as there may have been other factors impacting the difference.

The Army into which I was drafted, much like society, was not integrated. To the contrary: it was absolutely segregated, with the only exception being that there were senior white officers in African American units supervising the black junior officers. Contrast the US Army of 1944 with the Army of 1989, where four-star General Colin Powell, an African American, was the Commander of the US Army Forces Command (the largest US Army command based at Fort Bragg). General Powell later became chairman of the Joint Chiefs of Staff, and by US law, his position was the highest-ranking and senior most military officer in the United States Armed Forces and the principal military advisor to the President.

As of 2017, the US Army has a three-star General, Lt. General Nadja West an African American, the highest female ever to graduate from the US Military Academy at West Point. She is the US Army Surgeon General. An African American military officer who outranks General West is Michelle Howard, a four-star African American admiral, who is the commander of US Naval Forces Europe (at this writing). And then there is President Barak Obama, Commander in Chief of the United States of America Armed Forces—yes, the entire Army, Navy, Air Force, and Marines.

Time heals, but battle scars remain, and I still get irritated thinking about the abusive white officers of WWII.

My Second Tour of Duty

I got out of the Army in 1946 at the conclusion of the war. I was safe and never injured, but the war cost the US military 407,300 lives and an untold number of injuries. Even so, after two years I was ready for more green, so I reenlisted in 1948. My reentry point was Fort Dix, New Jersey, a place where I was to see my first television and my last official duty station. At Fort Dix, I had to go through military basic retraining to include re-qualifying with the weapon of choice at the time—still the M1.

During this second tour, I had the option of choosing a different career path. I could choose from either mechanic school (where most of the skilled African American recruits were assigned) or radio operator school. I chose radio school because I couldn't imagine being under vehicles (cars and trucks of various sizes) getting dirty and greasy. Even today, I loathe getting my hands dirty. Yes, I am a country boy, but no, I do not like getting my hands dirty. (Did vanity make me take this career path Probably!) Contrary to popular belief, country people have soap and water and know how to use them.

About the hand thing: I can remember back to high school where the girls always admired my hands, so naturally I wanted to keep them clean. I always kept my fingernails clean and manicured. My nails were thin, so it always looked as if I had nail polish on them. The girls always held my hands, but in reality, although I liked the attention, even more important for me was that I couldn't stand getting my hands dirty. I suppose clean hands are not something that one associates with being a macho soldier, but I had to have clean hands. Maybe this is because of my mother, who had a similar fetish.

Fort Monmouth

Fort Monmouth is located in the county of Monmouth, New Jersey and is where the US Army Radio School was located in 1948 and for a few years after the war ended. Fort Monmouth was the Signal Corps Training Center during WWII. In the two years I was out of the Army, the Army had seen little integration. At the radio school at Fort Monmouth, things would change somewhat. There were few African American soldiers in radio school—too few to have separate classes for us—so radio school was fully integrated, both in the classroom and in the barracks or dormitory. Not only was it integrated but blacks, to include myself, were in leadership roles. In fact, I was a squad leader, responsible for about ten soldiers/students. I was a squad leader for black and white troops, and yes, the white soldiers did obey my orders.

I gave orders relative to muster or transitioning from the barracks in uniform into a formal formation outside of the barracks and marching in formation. I was responsible for assigning soldiers to cleaning the barracks, preparing for inspections, giving supervisors reports, and a range of other tasks.

If you remember earlier, I indicated that I only got into one fight while in the military. Well, I almost got into another fight at Fort Monmouth. You see, I have always taken great pride in my appearance, and to this end, I was always the sharpest dresser in my units. My clothes were starched and creased, and my shoes were spit-shined, always the shiniest in the unit.

One day, one of the white soldiers I supervised made a statement about my shoes. He stated that my shoes were "as shiny as a nigger's shiny titty." I remember those words as clear as day. These were fighting words, and fortunately more level heads prevailed, and no fight ensued. We carried on, business as usual.

Fort Monmouth was a military base only a few miles—probably less than ten—from a town in New Jersey called Asbury Park, or Neptune. These were ocean towns where there was a boardwalk, restaurants, and nightclubs. I had family who lived in Neptune, so whenever I got weekend leave, I would head to town and meet up with my cousins and go out clubbing. My Aunt Ida had a daughter and two sons who frequently accompanied me to town. I also had schoolmates who migrated from Como, North Carolina, who had attended C. S. Brown High School with me, who were now living in Neptune.

Trainees at Fort Monmouth didn't have much transportation. I can't remember anyone ever having a car, so most often when I went to town from base I caught a bus, as did just about everyone else going to town. One evening, I stayed in town a little too long and missed the bus back to base, as did some white soldiers. We waited together at the bus stop for a taxi cab. We had been drinking, and there was this one guy from Georgia who was a real rebel. He was selling wolf tickets—talking smack, stating that when he got back to Georgia, he would be fighting and killing niggers all night long. He then looked at me and said, "You colored, aren't you?" At least he had the respect not to call me a nigger.

I responded with, "Yeah, I'm colored. What of it?" All the while, I was fingering a pocket knife, ready to strike. Carrying a pocket knife was just something everyone growing up in rural North Carolina did. It wasn't as much a weapon as it was a tool. Fortunately, I didn't have to use it. This rebel backed down with a little nudging from his friends. We then all got into the same taxi cab and were transported back to camp without further incident.

Despite these incidents, overall there was little racial strife between blacks and whites at Fort Monmouth.

My uncle, Lincoln Bryant, also lived nearby in Long Branch, and he came to visit me several times when I was at Fort Monmouth. Each time he visited, I was away from base. Lincoln was my mother's baby brother, and his mother died when he was seven years old. He and the rest of his siblings were disbursed among the adult relatives, and Lincoln was taken in and informally adopted by his uncle, who lived in New Jersey. His three sisters and two brothers remained in Suffolk, Virginia with relatives. Lincoln remained in New Jersey, never traveling south again for the next twenty years.

When Lincoln was 27 years old, one of his sisters died, and he returned home to Suffolk for her funeral. Prior to that, it is my understanding that not only did Lincoln not travel the 500 or so miles south during those 20 years but also none of his siblings traveled north during those years to visit him. Lincoln was loved by his adopted family in New Jersey and never seemed traumatized by the separation. He was just the most gentle and easy to get along with person one could ever meet. Once I got out of the military, Lincoln would visit me or my mother every year, and we always had a great time.

The most joyous thing that happened to me while I was stationed at Fort Monmouth was the birth of our oldest child, Edward, born in 1948. I couldn't take leave to travel home for his birth because I was in school, and the school was pretty demanding, but the more important reason that I couldn't take leave was that I wasn't allowed to. Edward was born on the 29th of August, and I knew that the Labor Day holiday was coming up, and I would get a few days off. As soon as we got off duty on Labor Day, I headed for the bus station and home. Before I left base, I knew that I would be punished when I returned because I had planned to stay an extra day, and knew this would be considered AWOL, absence without leave. Sure enough, my sergeant gave me hell upon my return and three days of kitchen patrol (KP). It was worth it.

Becoming A Radio Operator

A radio operator at the time had to know Morse code because that was the primary means of secure communication back then (secure communication is a type of coded communication, which the enemy will not be able to decode). Not only did I have to learn Morse code but I also had to learn to translate the code into English, and then type the English translation so that other soldiers in other units would be able decode and understand my transmissions. This meant that I learned the Morse code system and to type at the same time.

I and my fellow classmates leaned to type on a blind typewriter (a typewriter that has no letters or numbers on the keys). In order to graduate with low proficiency, one had to type 25 words (a word is five alphabetic characters) in one minute. Five characters of DAHs or DITs—a series of dots or dashes—would equal one alphabet. So, in order to type 25 words, we had to listen to up to125 DAHs and DITs, and we couldn't make more than five mistakes. I graduated as a highly proficient coder, being able to type a coded 40 words a minute.

This was an exceedingly challenging school, requiring us to listen to codes through earphones and the constant coding, DAHs and DITs could be maddening. It was nothing to see someone snatch off their earphones and throw them against the floor or wall and storm out of the room. Our attrition rate in this portion of radio school alone was greater than 50%, and here I was a highly proficient Morse Code graduate.

At radio operator school, we were taught the different types of radios used by the Army, along with how to tune them to a specific frequency/channel, string antennas, and that kind of stuff. Learning to operate the radios was not difficult, and this was a piece of cake compared to learning Morse Code.

After six months of schooling at Fort Monmouth, we graduated and were officially radiomen. Radiomen serve in all branches of the military, and after graduation, I would no longer be assigned to an artillery unit; instead, I would be going to an infantry unit. Yes, I would become a ground fighting soldier. An infantry soldier was something that I did not want to be, and almost as soon as I arrived at my new unit, I began plotting ways of getting out.

I left Fort Monmouth, New Jersey on the east coast for Fort Lewis, Washington on the west coast. Today, Fort Lewis is called Joint Base Lewis McChord. More than fifty years later, my grandson and namesake, Henian, would follow me to Fort Lewis, which is where he would prepare for war in Afghanistan.

When I left Fort Monmouth and returned to the real Army, it was once again to a segregated all-black unit. However, the regular Army had changed a little, and because of the change at my next unit, we would be commanded by a black lieutenant colonel, a guy by the name of Chase, Lt. Colonel Hyman Y. Chase. He was a senior officer. I think that he was from somewhere up north, maybe around Washington, DC or Baltimore, Maryland, but I am not sure. If he was from the Washington, DC area, I imagine that he might have graduated from Howard or maybe the Morgan State University ROTC program, where years later my grandson, Henian, would obtain his college degree and be commissioned into the US Army.

Chase, like Lt. Jones and Cherry, was a tough, demanding officer. Certainly, his reputation preceded him to the point that when word came down that he was coming to our post, everybody was hoping that he was going to an artillery outfit. He could have gone to an artillery or infantry unity because he was both an infantry and artillery officer. As luck would have it, we got him.

Now before Lt. Colonel Chase got to Fort Lewis, I had been assigned to a headquarters unit. Headquarters are typically the unit for senior officers, chief honchos, and that would be Lt. Colonel Chase office. Lt. Colonel Chase had a no-nonsense attitude to the point that he was feared more than the white officers. Certainly, he made you think of a mature Lt. Jones or Cherry.

There was another African American officer at Fort Lewis, and we always called him Iron Jaw. Not to his face, of course, because it was a nickname. Captain Eldridge Carter was assigned the nickname Iron Jaw not because he could take a punch to the jaw but because he talked so much. Iron Jaw always had something to say. Iron Jaw was a soldier's soldier, as he came in for revelry every single day, unlike most officers. When I say every day, I mean every day—to include the weekends. On Sunday mornings after church, you could expect to see Iron Jaw. Captain Carter, Iron Jaw, was one of the early casualties of the Korean War.

Back to my first assignment out of radio school. I was assigned not for my proficiency with the radio but because of the typing skills I had acquired at radio school. I was not a radioman; I was a clerk typist. Six months' specialty training, and they make me a clerk typist. As they say, only in America.

As a clerk, I was at least stationary and didn't have to go out on infantry training maneuvers. Infantry soldiers stay out in the field, eating C rations, and rarely get a chance to take baths. They train day and night in all sorts of weather. You see, in war, you can't always choose the conditions under which you fight. Yes, I unapologetically preferred remaining in the rear on base when they went out on field maneuvers. This didn't last long, however.

At Fort Lewis, as mentioned, I was initially assigned as a clerk typist but soon found myself in a "grunt" infantry unit working as a radio operator for a demanding supervisor. I became the radioman for Lt. Colonel Chase. I was leaving Paradise, New Jersey, where I had been for the previous 30 weeks in school sleeping indoors, on sheets, in bed every night, eating in the mess hall, to join an infantry unit—sleeping outside, walking miles at a time, and eating C rations (meals out of cans).

Before I go on, I must tell you how I came to work for Lt. Colonel Chase. Lt. Colonel Chase was a busy body, and when on maneuvers, he was assigned a jeep and a personal radioman to maintain communication with his subordinates—a couple of thousand soldiers who were at great distances. On maneuvers, he was on foot as much as in his jeep, in and out of that jeep. Getting in and out of that jeep was very challenging for a radioman, who was responsible for an approximately 25-pound radio. A radioman had to lug a radio on his back, put the radio on and take it off, secure the radio and antenna to the jeep, and so on. Well, one night, Lt. Colonel Chase's radioman got lost, and he fired him the next day. Guess who replaced the fired radioman? You got it, me. The first thing Lt. Colonel Chase told me was, "Newsome, you better not lose me, or I will fire your ass, too." So, I made sure that any time we had night maneuvers, a time where I would most likely get separated from Lt. Colonel Chase, that I camped out in my sleeping bag right next to his jeep. On the one occasion when I chose to let Lt. Colonel Chase know how inconvenient it was to be getting in and out of the jeep with the radio, he informed me, "Hell, it ain't inconvenient for me, and your ass better not get lost." I didn't.

While at Fort Lewis, I was able to visit Hawaii, although it wasn't a real vacation. The unit went there on a training mission—war games, where the Army, Navy, and Air Corps trained for an amphibious landing. We left Fort Lewis for San Diego, California, where we boarded landing craft and transferred to a large, troop-carrying ship by scaling the side of the ship on web ropes draped along the side of the ship. Once in Hawaii, we did the reverse maneuver—we scaled/climbed down the side of the ship on the web rope ladder, dropped into landing craft, and stormed the beach. Then we marched in formation to our barracks.

We trained in Hawaii for a total of a partial day, but we stayed in Hawaii for a full week taking in the sights. Fifty years later, my granddaughter (Dawn), grandson-in-law, and great-grandson (Caleb) would live in Hawaii.

On the way back from Hawaii to the States, the Navy and Air Corp continued to train, but there was little formal training for us. We spent much of our day and night in the bottom half of the ship.

Back at Fort Lewis, we continued training, but I was transferred out a few months later, just before the entire unit shipped out for Korea. The 1st Calvary stationed in Japan at the time would be the first to arrive to Korea for the fight. My former unit at Fort Lewis, the 2nd Division, was the first unit to transfer out of the United States as the outbreak of hostilities in Korea (Korea was never classified as a war) escalated. The 2nd Division indeed would follow the 1st Calvary Division into the fight in Korea. The 2nd Division took extremely heavy causalities during the conflict and in one battle alone lost a third of its soldiers. The estimated the number of Korean War casualties for the 2nd Division was 7,432 killed in action; 16,575 wounded in action; and 338 who died of wounds. In the entire conflict, there were 33,686 US military deaths.

As I said, I was fortunate, as I had transferred to Ft Ord, California one week before the unit deployed. I remained at Fort Ord for about two months, and then I went to radar repair training for about 31 weeks. Radar repair school was housed at Fort Bliss, Texas right outside of El Paso on the boarder of Mexico and the city of Jaquez. The two cities are separated by the Rio Grande River. As mentioned, I never wanted to be in the infantry, and from day one, I applied for anything that could get me out of the infantry, which meant mostly applying for different military schools. My persistence eventually paid off, and I avoided the worst part of the Korean Conflict when I got assigned to radar repair school.

It was at Fort Lewis that I thought I would have my family with me for the first time since I joined the Army, and Essie Nora and I got us a little place. Not long after she arrived at Fort Lewis, I got orders to travel to Fort Ord, California in the Monterey Bay area so Essie Nora and I headed south. In California, we rented a place in Sea Side, I believe not far from San Francisco. Edward remained in Ahoskie with Essie Nora's mother. We had planned on bringing him out once we got settled, but within weeks of arriving, I got orders for radar repair school in Fort Bliss, Texas, so Essie Nora returned home to Ahoskie.

Radar repair school is where one learns to fix radars. Really, what we learned about was electronics, electronics, and more electronics. This school was math intensive. During the first week, we learned arithmetic, algebra, geometry, trigonometry, slide rule, and the power-of-ten. We didn't have calculators or computers. The most advanced tool we had was the slide rule which I don't even think you can purchase today—it is outdated like abacuses are. In reality, you had to know this information before beginning the school because that first week was really only a review.

I didn't completely avoid the Korean Conflict. In 1951 after completing radar repair school, I was sent to Korea and stayed there for 10 months. I was not sent to Korea to repair radars, my most recent specialty, but to operate radios and to transmit communication using Morse Code. I hadn't forgotten it, although I had not used it in almost three years. Still, it was deeply embedded in my subconscious.

The expected tour in Korea was 15 months, but my enlistment expired at 10 months, and I elected to leave the war zone to return home to Winton/Ahoskie and get out of the military again. I was discharged in 1952 but would only be out of the military for about a month. I would reenlist in 1952 for my third enlistment. During my second enlistment, I spent 60 weeks—more than a year—in two different schools lasting about 30 weeks each.

Fort Rucker — Alabama

When I got out of the military in 1952, I only stayed out for about one month and then processed right back in through Fort Jackson, South Carolina. Fort Jackson is where my youngest son Douglas would complete basic combat training years later, and his son, Henian, would complete basic officers' training school. Although I was only out of the Army for a month, I had to reprocess and get some refresher training, which included going back through the gas chamber—something I hated in basic and something I dreaded even more this time. I remember the misery associated with going into a gas chamber—pulling our mask off, breathing in those toxic chemicals, and then for me and just about everyone else, puking my guts out.

After a few weeks at Fort Jackson, I was assigned to Fort Gordon, Georgia, back in a signal corps unit but where there was not a slot for my rank. Since there was no slot for me, they assigned me to work as an instructor for radio operators.

I was stationed at Fort Gordon for such a short period of time that I can't remember much about it. From Fort Gordon I would be transferred to Fort Rucker, Alabama.

MOLASSES, FATBACK, AND BISCUITS

The best thing to happen for Essie Nora, myself, and Edward in Alabama was the birth of Marcus. Marcus wasn't born in Alabama; he was born in Ahoskie, as Essie Nora had traveled back to Ahoskie during the latter part of her pregnancy for family support, something many military wives did at the time. Although there was local support, nothing compares with the support of one's family and particularly one's mother during pregnancy, I am told.

At Fort Rucker, Alabama, I was assigned to the Regimental Command, which was another infantry unit, and as I always did when I was assigned to an infantry unit, I began searching for an escape.

A transfer out of the unit didn't come immediately, and while I was at Fort Rucker, a US Army MOS survey team came through to determine whether soldiers were properly assigned, I was not. The survey team determined that I was working below my service and training grade and not in my radar repair rating, as I should have been. I was reassigned to an artillery unit, and that, of course, was okay by me. I became a communication chief for the unit. My rank was Sergeant First Class, E-7, the second highest enlisted rank in the Army, but two years later, they added a couple of more enlisted grades/ranks, E-8 and E-9.

Nuclear Weapons

In January 1954, I was reassigned again. This time, I would be going to Sandia Air Force Base in Albuquerque, New Mexico, where we were to add the final two children to our family, Douglas and Sheila. Sandia Air Force Base was a nuclear weapons unit, and I would be working on those weapons/bombs. How did I get assigned to nuclear weapons? Well, as I have previously stated, anytime I was assigned to an infantry unit, the first thing I began to do was plot an exit strategy. My basic exit strategy from Fort Rucker was by applying for any type of training or schools that I could get. One of the schools I applied to was nuclear weapons school, although I really had little idea of what I was getting myself into. Anyway, many months after I put in my application for the nuclear school at Sandia Air Force base, I got orders to report. I suppose that it took an extremely long time for me to be notified because of the extensive background check they did on me in order for me to get a top-secret clearance.

At Sandia Air Force Base, I was no longer in a segregated unit. I was now in a "near segregated unit," where there were only three blacks in the unit. There was me, working on nuclear bombs, an African American cook, and an African American mechanic.

I was stationed at Sandia Air Force Base for approximately three years, in school and then for permanent party. I learned to test and make sure the wires connecting the various components of the weapon were serviceable. I learned to inspect the weapon to make sure the explosive didn't leak and generally to calibrate the serviceability of the weapon. The bombs were called "Little Boy," "Fat Man," or "Marc 6." The Little Boy was the bomb that was dropped on Japan, which helped bring WWII to an end.

While at Sandia Air Force Base, I was temporarily reassigned to Fort Sill, Oklahoma in 1955 (where my youngest son would be stationed 20 years later) but returned to Albuquerque a few months later. It was in Oklahoma where we got our first television, about seven years after I had first seen a television. Our television was a black and white that received three channels at the most. Even so, owning a television was big time.

My entire unit was transferred from Sandia Air Force Base to upstate New York, and we landed at Seneca Ordinance Depot, Seneca, New York. Seneca Ordinance Depot is where the US Army began storing nuclear weapons with our unit's arrival. We didn't live in Seneca, however, we lived in a little town called Waterloo, New York. When we arrived, we became only the second African American family living in the city.

We lived in Waterloo for maybe two years, and our two oldest children, Edward and Marcus, were the only black children in their class—and maybe the entire school. I assumed Edward was safe in school, as he was older and could take care of himself, spending his early years in Ahoskie. Certainly, he never suggested that he was having problems. Marcus was younger, and I am not sure what went on after the doors of the school closed, but we had a dog, Rusty, who escorted Marcus to and from school every day. At about the time the school would be letting out, old Rusty would head out to go escort his companion home, I don't know how Rusty learned how to tell time but he did. We were not able to take Rusty on our next assignment to Germany, so we left him with family. Unfortunately, he got hit by a car and killed while we were away.

From Seneca, our unit shipped out to Germany, to a military base at Pirmasens. Again, this was a nuclear ordinance depot. My family accompanied me to Germany, where the oldest two sons attended school, the youngest son attended kindergarten, and the youngest child, Sheila, stayed at home. We had no television there, so when I was home, we had a lot of family time. All three of the boys—Edward, Marcus, and Douglas—learned to play chess while we were living in Germany, and on Saturday mornings, the boys went to the movies to see the Batman series.

A couple of times a month, Essie Nora and I socialized with other military couples. Most of the time, the couple was composed of a US Soldier and his German girlfriend. Also, on Sundays, the family would typically go into town, sightseeing. We had an old station wagon, and the kids always kidded that there were areas in the floor that were so rusted out, one could see the road.

New MOS Supply

My next duty station was Korea, an unaccompanied hardship tour where I was assigned to another Nuclear Weapons Unit—again, an ordinance unit. At about the time I arrived to the unit, somebody had committed suicide. I think that it was a captain who had gotten word that his wife wanted a divorce and had a boyfriend. As was customary at the time, and I believe today, someone had to accompany the body home. The person tasked with accompanying the body home was the supply sergeant because he was due to rotate out of Korea in the near future. Because the supply sergeant had rotated out, and I was awaiting clearance again, I was tasked with the job. I took the Supply MOS training and then tested, passed it, and was assigned the job permanently. I would remain a supply sergeant the remainder of my time in the military, which was fine with me. Supply was pretty laid back and was a position where a lot of socialization occurred, so I enjoyed it.

After Korea, Fort Benning, Georgia was my next duty station, and I would be stationed there for three years. Fort Benning is the home of the US Army Airborne School. This tour was really impactful on at least one of my sons, the eldest, Edward, to the point that he would return for Airborne training himself less than five years later. Unlike me, Edward was not only Airborne but was also an infantry soldier.

In Georgia, we were about four hundred miles from Winton, North Carolina, and recruits were pouring into the Army because of the draft and the Vietnam War. It was at Fort Benning, Georgia that I was stationed with more of my home boys at one time than I ever had before; there was Buddy Holloman (Essie Nora's cousin), Billy Simmons, and Clyde Everett. We hung out occasionally at the club, and they would stop by the house.

Georgia was/is deep in the south, and in the early '60s, a period of racial turmoil saw Georgia in all of its racial glory and hatred. There was significant violence in the streets, as African Americans were marching in public for basic human, but also equal rights, but the police were insistent that they would flex their muscle. Police beat the marchers merciless with billy clubs and turned water hoses and German Shepherds loose on the peaceful marchers. No, the south was not a pleasant place for an African American to be during the early '60s.

Things were a little better on base, and there was the occasional white NCO who wanted to make it clear that he was not a racist. I can remember one night at the club where we were drinking, and this one white guy from the unit had his daughter and her boyfriend. He insisted that I dance with his daughter, I reluctantly agreed and that was that. Out in the community, I likely would have been lynched for such behavior. So, since it was safer on post than in the community, the family didn't have much contact with the community other than by television, as we rarely ventured off base.

The most memorable thing I remember about work at Fort Benning was that my boys were old enough that I could invite them to work with me, and they were thrilled to actually hold military rifles and pistols and talk with the other soldiers in the unit. Also, as mentioned, Fort Benning was/is home to the US Army Airborne School and a place where other NATO countries come to train. One country that sent troops to train was Cuba, and the Cuban officers and I did a lot of bartering, as I was a supply officer. I think that I benefited the most personally from this exchange, as I was a cigar smoker and, as part of any trade we made, I received Cuban cigars. I viewed this as an excellent partnership.

From Georgia, I received orders back to Korea, my third tour there. In my last overseas tour of duty, I would have to get physical with one of my troops, but I wouldn't call it a fight. On this particular occasion, I was just doing my job. I was a sergeant in charge of the base on the evening/midnight shift and had to go into the village and conduct patrols but happened to be in the office at this time. The base was adjacent to a little Korean village that had bars and such, and soldiers would go into town at night, have fun, drink, and let off steam. On this particular night, one of the little Korean boys who hung around the base came running into my office screaming that American soldiers were fighting at the Gateway Bar. It was about 2300 hours, curfew for soldiers and time for them to be back on base, as the base gates were soon to be locked.

I ran down to the Gateway and proceeded to break up the fight, and in the process had to pull one of the combatants off the other and take him to the ground. The reason we got into the tussle was because the guy attempted to grab my weapon, a .45-caliber pistol, and this was absolutely a no-no. When I got him to the ground, he attempted to strike me with his fist. I looked him in the eye and told him to take his best shot. Well, he might have been intoxicated, but he knew better than to strike an NCO. For his behavior, he was court marshaled, fined, and reduced in rank. Today, such behavior would get you booted out of the military—but it didn't during Vietnam.

From Korea, I had orders to Germany, back to a foreign duty station, and I was getting a very uncomfortable feeling about those orders. Vietnam was hot, and it seemed that everyone was being sent there. Germany was a debarkation station for many soldiers heading to Vietnam, and I felt that I was likely to get orders to Vietnam before my tour in Germany was over. It was my belief, true or not, that I was Vietnam bound.

After 20 years in the Army, I did not want to be on the front lines or even in the rear of a war that was being waged primarily in the jungles of Southeast Asia. Vietnam was looking very bloody in my eyes, and indeed there would be 58,220 US military deaths in Vietnam. I was 40 years old and couldn't see myself in Vietnam getting injured or, worse, killed.

No, I was not trying to die in Vietnam, so I began planning to get out of the Army and retire. Getting from Korea back home proved difficult. The trip from Korea to California and then Chicago, Illinois was fine, but when we got to Chicago, there was a pilots' strike, and civilian airlines were grounded. Myself and my traveling companion, another sergeant coming from Korea, contacted the local Air Force Base as a last hope for a quick trip home. We were able to get a military hop in the back of a C-130 cargo plane from Chicago to New Jersey, and then we caught a bus home.

I can't remember the name of my traveling companion, but he was from Petersburg, Virginia, which was maybe 100 miles north of Ahoskie. He also had orders to Germany and wanted nothing to do with that assignment, so we decided to meet up in a couple of days while on leave and travel to the Pentagon to see whether we could get our orders changed. On the designated day, I drove up to Petersburg, and this guy's girlfriend drove us to Alexandria, Virginia and then to the Pentagon.

Once in the Pentagon, we began asking everyone we saw about getting our orders changed and had no luck. As we prepared to leave, we met a sergeant who knew my companion. Relationships are oh so important. This sergeant, who used to be responsible for enlisted duty assignments and movement, was now assigned to officer duty assignments and movement. We explained our dilemma, and he said, "Give me your orders, go get a cup of coffee, and meet me back here in an hour." In that hour, he was able to get our orders changed. I was to report to Fort Dix, New Jersey, and my companion was to report to Fort Lee, Virginia—right in his backyard. Fort Dix would be my last assignment before I retired.

I escaped the military injury free when, during the course of my 21 years of service, there were a total of 499,206 military deaths—that's a half-million deaths and an untold number of injured as a result of wars and conflicts.

When I left the Army, I had the following ribbons:

CBI — China Burma India; Western Pacific Campaign, with Battle Stars
Asia Pacific Theater Service Medal, with two Bronze Service Stars
Korean Ribbon, with Battle Stars
World War II Victory Medal
Good Conduct

I suppose that I have a military legacy in that two of my three sons, Edward and Douglas, served in the US Army, and two of Douglas's sons served in the military—Douglas Jr. in the US Air Force and Henian in the US Army.

MOLASSES, FATBACK, AND BISCUITS

Me getting ready for town, a little R&R

Me headed to town again, but I have some time to chat

On maneuvers – Ft. Lewis, Washington

And then there was supply

Civilian Life

My first job out of the military was driving taxicabs. I worked for Branch Taxi. Driving taxicabs was a job where one gets to meet every kind of person; however, in small towns, unlike large cities, there was a specific demographic who utilized taxi services. The people who use taxies in Ahoskie were mostly poor, as every middle or upper middle-class person/family in Ahoskie, I believe, owned a vehicle back then.

During the day, I picked up people making grocery runs, or maybe needing to go to the Social Security office, or the doctor's office or hospital, or maybe the nine or ten miles to visit a relative in the county jail. In the evenings and on weekends, a majority of my trips were to establishments where alcohol was involved—bars or clubs, or the liquor (ABC) store in Powellsville, North Carolina, which was located in Bertie County. Ahoskie did not have a liquor store, and country people drink. Just as popular as legal establishments that sold liquor were speakeasies, and "bootlegger joints," and you can bet my customers knew where they were located. Soon, I knew where they were located, also.

Yes, my main runs were related to alcohol and party events. I transported people down to east end, to Grady Shamebley, Sam Pillman, Raleigh Demery, and on Highway 13, the Casaymia. For some reason, people were as likely to request trips to bootlegger joints way out in the boonies as to established places. The bootleggers sold state liquor as well as the stuff made in the woods in the local stills.

There was a lone local African American constable/police officer patrolling Ahoskie and surrounding areas named Abner Sessoms. He was Ahoskie's first black police officer, and he knew everyone in the area, to include legal café owners, nightclub owners, and illegal bootleggers. They say that he was on the take. I don't know, but that was the gossip in Ahoskie and surrounding areas for a long, long time. I don't know how Abner got his job, but he owned a pool hall before being selected to be a police officer. Maybe owning a pool hall helped him understand the criminal elements, as many people suggested that Ahoskie pool halls were fronts for gambling and selling liquor. I don't know for sure because I didn't go into the pool hall that much, but there was plenty of gossip about Abner, his pool hall, and his brother, Chic.

Abner was a pretty tough guy. He reportedly killed a boy in the line of duty. I don't know why he shot the boy, but he did.

I worked as a taxicab driver for maybe 12 months. I then took a job as a factory worker at the aluminum plant in Winton, located on the Chowan River, where I worked for about a year. I departed the Aluminum Plant for the chemical plant, also on the Chowan River, where I checked samples of waters, monitored meters, and tested water leaving the plant and returning to the river.

I left the Chemical Plant for a government job with the Norfolk Naval Base. I first commuted the 70 miles one way to the Navy Base. I would drive 40 miles and then catch a bus the remaining 30 miles. Driving in fog, which was a regular occurrence, especially in the early morning, and avoiding deer always kept me alert and on my toes. There was a period of time when my family was in Ahoskie, and I roomed with my dad's sister, Ethel Watts, until my family moved up to Portsmouth.

At the Naval Base, I was a warehouse worker loading supplies on Navy ships preparing for deployment. It was in this job where I was injured and out of work for the first time in my life. I had been in the Army and went on sick call only three times—once because of trouble with my wisdom teeth. At the Naval Base, a forklift hit my foot, breaking a bone in the inner foot. If I had not had on leather work boots, I am sure the accident would have taken my foot off.

My last job was with the US Post Officer in Portsmouth, Virginia. I worked as a letter carrier for the next seven years. First as a substitute, where I didn't have a permanent route. My first official route was delivering mail in the Churchland area of Portsmouth, and then I got a route delivering mail in the Cavalier Manor neighborhood of Portsmouth. Cavalier Manor was the part of the city where upper middle class African Americans lived. At the time, I delivered mail to two prominent military families living in Cavalier Manor; one was a boy from Bertie County, Lt. Colonel Fred Cherry (not the same Cherry from BCT). Lt. Colonel Cherry was a former Air Force pilot who had been shot down and become a prisoner of war (POW) in Vietnam for seven years. The other was a guy by the name of Carl Brashear, a retired master chief petty officer, the first African American Master Diver in the United States Navy. The movie *Men of Honor* was made about his life story.

The thing that I remember most about the post office were the dogs, who never wanted me to deliver mail to their houses. Small or large, none seemed to like mailmen, or at least they didn't seem to like me. On occasion, I would let my guard down and get bitten. This was the downside of the job. Also, I remember the workload studies management imposed on us letter carriers; the post office was about being as efficient as possible, and they needed to ensure that we were making the best of our time.

About once every three years, a manager would tag along with us on our routes for a couple of days to see how long it took us to deliver the mail. Well, these studies didn't seem to benefit management, at least in my opinion, because whenever we had a workload study, we the letter carriers did everything in our power to prolong the day and broke no rules, none. We never cut a corner or walked across grass, and although we knew numerous shortcuts, you can bet that we never took a shortcut doing these periods. We milked the clock for everything it was worth. So personally, I can't see how they used the workload study for their benefit.

The absolute best thing about being a letter carrier was meeting people and developing relationships. I developed relationships with other letter carriers and postal clerks. I met family members I hadn't seen in years, my children's friends, and their parents. I developed relationships with children, teenagers, young adults, middle-age adults, as welled as aged individuals. Many of these individuals seemed to look forward to my almost daily visit, depending on whether or not they got mail on a given day.

On the Cavalier Manor route, I was responsible for delivering mail to Tower Mall and developed relationships with merchants, clerks, and security. With the technological revolution and communication occurring through gadgets, I don't see how we as humans can maintain our humanity. Many, many of the homes to which I delivered mail found it in their hearts to remember me on Christmas, making sure that I got a gift.

Delivering mail is a job of course, and I went through shoes and socks frequently, as I put lots of miles on my feet—rain, snow, sleet, hail, freezing temperature, hot, humid, scorching temperature, the mail was delivered. In the end, however, it was a job I loved.

Life was not all work and no play in Portsmouth, as there were many activities to engage in. I frequently attended Virginia Squires basketball games played at the Scope in Norfolk and watched the great Dr. Julius Erving, Larry Brown, Doug Moe, and George Gervin. We attended amateur and professional boxing matches, and we visited and entertained friends and family. I have always loved fishing, and we would visit Harrison's Pier in the Oceanview section of Norfolk and piers in Virginia Beach. Essie Nora and I also went to dances as frequently as possible.

We would eventually leave Portsmouth and return full circle to Ahoskie, North Carolina to spend the majority of our days sitting on the porch, where we would entertain family, friends, and yes, even strangers.

Son Marcus' rendition of me as a postal clerk

Retirement in Ahoskie

Essie Nora and I enjoyed being home again where family was close by. The children were a little farther away, but the farthest child was only maybe 200 miles away. We enjoyed eating country food right out of the garden, visiting, and just sitting on our large porch, just like the old days. In the south, sitting on the porch attracts flies and mosquitoes, but more importantly, neighborly people. People didn't have to call in advance or have an invitation; they could and would just stop by and socialize. We always had time for company and really enjoyed having guests. This was the life, and yes, after traveling the globe, I had little desire to travel anymore.

Essie Nora got sick with Alzheimer's in about 2005, and in 2015 the love of my life passed. She didn't pass in a foreign nursing home but in her home. After spending 60 plus years of your life with someone, their passing takes a toll, but she lives in my heart and in my memories, and I am surrounded by family and friends. Indeed, Essie Nora was a strong woman. She raised four children, who all obtained college degrees—three obtained doctoral degrees. All three boys are still married to their original wives, and all have been married at least 30 years. Her daughter, a lovely woman, has achieved much in her own right. I like to say that I didn't find Essie Nora, she found me. I was oh-so-fortunate that she did.

Yes, Essie Nora loved people, family, and friends. She loved to talk. She had a life-long love of music and dance, and on a daily basis would visit one of her nephews, an Ahoskie bootlegger who played oldies, the music she loved. Essie Nora was not much of a drinker, so she would have a pop and just socialize with the crowd.

Jeopardy! and *Wheel of Fortune* were her favorite television shows, and she made it a point to be home before these shows came on.

After she passed, I continued to be supported by my three sons, Edward, Marcus, Douglas, and daughter, Sheila; their spouses, Saundra, Patsy, Esther, Sylvester; ten grandchildren, Lynnell, Kyndess, Henian, Marcus, Douglas, Henian, Dawn, Phillip, Dana, Jasmine; and nine great-grandchildren, Nehemiah, Noah, Jason, Caleb, Jayden, Jonah, Carmen, Jordan, and Joshua.

Me, Essie Nora, children, and their spouses. Not listed are grandchildren and great-grandchildren

We are Family

The Church

In rural northeast North Carolina, most African American families attended church. Likewise, my family and I attended church regularly. I was raised a Southern Baptist and brought up in the Baptist Church, and we believe in the Lord and Savior Jesus Christ. We were a praying family, especially at mealtime. Dad, being the head of the family, would typically say the grace if he were home; otherwise, it was me, Bob, Mom, or a house guest. Any of us would say grace. I said a fairly simple grace and still say it today. My grace goes as follows: "Dear Lord, I thank you for this food that I am about to take for the nourishment of my body, forever—Amen."

I have also learned the Lord's Prayer, which I suppose I learned from word-of-mouth early on as a young child. The version I learned was the King James version:

> Our Father which art in heaven,
> hallowed be thy name.
> Thy kingdom come, thy will be done in earth,
> as it is in heaven.
> Give us this day our daily bread.

And forgive us our debts, as we forgive our debtors.
And lead us not into temptation, but deliver us from
evil: For thine is the kingdom, and the power, and
the glory, forever. Amen.

And my bedtime prayer went as follows:

Now I lay me down to sleep, if I die before I wake—
pray the Lord my soul to take—
happy Jesus' sake. Amen.

Early on, Bob and I were not members of but attended Mt. Mariah Church regularly, mostly Sundays. I think that the regular meeting was once a month. I believe that Dr. Calvin S. Brown was the pastor of Mt. Mariah Church when we attended. Of course, we got to church the same way we got anywhere—we walked. I imagine that we walked maybe three or four miles each way to church, and we never gave it a second thought. We went to church as a family, although Dad would attend a bit more than Mom.

I also attended Pleasant Plain Baptist church for a couple of years, and Pleasant Plains is where I was baptized in the Chowan River when I was about 13 or 14 years old. I never changed churches, so I suspect that I am still a member of Pleasant Plains. I think that Moses Newsome was the Pastor of Pleasant Plains when I was there. Moses Newsome was the father of Dr. Moses Newsome, who served at one time as the Dean of Social Work at Norfolk State University, the alma mater of two of my children, Douglas and Sheila.

After Andrew and I left home, Mom and Dad began attending Jordan Grove Church. Dad was active in the church; he was a sexton, church caretaker, or janitor and also served as treasurer.

When I think about the church today, the things that comes to my mind are mainly the ministers' responsibility to advocate for poor people. I believe and hope that most ministers are honest, but I am sure there are those who have other agendas. Honest or not, money seems to be on the agendas of many if not most pastors, and like most people, ministers can be tempted by money. First, I don't believe that most pastors are going to accept jobs that don't pay them what they expect to get paid. It's just a fact of life that most people are out to get as much money as possible, the clergy included. People very rarely do things altruistically these days, not even ministers, I don't believe. It is about the money, and once people get too much money, they often become corrupt.

Despite this fact, I do believe that people, to include ministers, are good and do bad things because they do not have high enough self-esteem. Unfortunately, when people grow up in certain environments, they are more likely to have low self-esteem and are more tempted to do wrong, including the clergy.

Politics

When I think about politics, the first thing I think about today is something that occurred in 2008. I absolutely didn't believe that it would happen, but it did: The United States of America elected Barak Obama President. No, I believed that in 2008, years after civil rights laws were enacted, this country was still extremely overtly and covertly racist. Sure, we had made progress but not that much. No, I did not believe that there would be enough whites to vote for him to push him over the top. I was wrong. He could not have gotten enough Black, Hispanic, or other minority votes to elect him President. The number of whites that voted for him were surly not a majority, but there were enough.

I am old school and just like blacks are set in their ways, whites are set in their ways. I don't believe that most whites have changed their hearts when it comes to my brethren. Nevertheless, today, there are clearly a number, although a minority, of liberal-thinking white people when it comes to race relations, and that is movement in the right direction. However, with the election of Donald Trump in 2016, there is also clearly a large number of white racist/white supremacists who care little about anyone of color, at least in my opinion. The sad thing is that I believe many of these individuals are educated.

I was aware that Douglas Wilder, an African American, got elected governor of the state of Virginia 20 years prior to President Obama's elections and that Virginia was/is traditionally a very conservative, southern state full of prejudice. In Virginia, politicians closed the public schools for 14 years rather than to integrate African American children and white children. However, I thought that the election of Douglas Wilder was a fluke and could not be repeated on a national level. I am glad that I was wrong.

President Obama's election the second time surprised me even more than his election the first time. I didn't believe that he would be elected the second time because the liberal whites who voted for him the first time were probably "fence sitters" and didn't think that their vote would be as pronounced the second time around. I thought that they wanted to prove to themselves that they were not racist—but even today, I suspect that some of those who voted for him still have some prejudice in their hearts. But that's okay, I am sure I do, too. It is a good thing that they voted for him regardless of their rational. Being half-racist is better than being 75%, 85%, or 100% racist, as I see it. On the other hand, I can't fathom an African American *not* voting for Barak Obama—even the good-old boy Colin Powell deserted the Republican Party to vote for then Mr. Obama.

When I was in the military, there was a white guy in Georgia—I guess he was from Georgia—who was always trying to convince me that he was not a racist. He tried to portray himself, as best he could, that there was not a prejudice bone in his body. This meant that he went out of his way to associate with the blacks in the unit, as much as he could. He was very open about not being racist and prejudiced, so he did associate with us, which was the exception for white people at the time and probably put him and his family at risk given the climate of the early 1960s. I remember that I was at the non-commissioned officer's club on Fort Benning one night when he was there with his adult daughter and her husband. As mentioned before, his daughter and her husband danced a little bit, and he kept telling me to go ahead and dance with his daughter—someone else's wife—without getting permission from either her or her husband.

I felt really uncomfortable, but after being pushed, I did ask the husband if it was okay. He gave permission, and we danced. Can you imagine an African American dancing with a white woman in Georgia in 1961? That was unquestionably a hanging offense at the time. Maybe that family and others weren't as prejudiced back then as I thought. Hell, I would like to think that he even voted for President Obama. I do believe that it is because I am a very fair-skinned African American. I imagine that if I were darker, it would not have happened that way.

However, as I think back on the last 50 years, racism today is not nearly as prevalent as it used to be—but rest assured, there is still racism. Prejudice and racism has been around forever; it exists around the world, in all cultures. There is prejudice in the African American community, where there is conflict between lighter-skinned and darker-skinned individuals. In my opinion, I feel that at its roots, all racism/prejudice is based on ignorance.

I believe for sure that school integration may have practically been responsible for President Obama's election because integration brings people together. White and black folks who would not have ever come together except they were forced together by school integration. This certainly is a good thing to come out of integration. We have a long way to go, though, because there are many, many other sociocultural barriers that foster racism. Until we can change family/cultural values, and the effect of keeping a class of people subservient, the impact of putting people together in schools will be minimal.

I remember the semi-moderate Romney, who was the governor of Massachusetts. He quickly changed his stripes to an extreme conservatism for personal and political gain. He developed a hard, inflexible attitude about African Americans and Hispanics, and his attitude fostered people to continue in their racist ways. And I will not even comment on the overt/covert messages of racism coming out of the mouth of Donald Trump other than to say it is amazing how naive some people can be. Electing Donald was like letting the fox in the hen house—or listening to the rabbit pleading to be thrown into the briar patch.

I follow politics much more today as an elder than I did as a young man. I cannot tell you when I began following politics. My parents certainly did not vote, or at least I never knew of them voting, and they never discussed voting with me. If my dad had voted, he would have talked about it with me because we got along great and talked about everything.

As a child, adolescent, and young adult, I was not aware of anyone in my neighborhood ever voting. Even after I went into the Army, I was not consciously aware of the importance of voting, nor did I vote or know anyone else who voted.

In the south where I grew up, there was a conscious attempt to prevent black people in particular from voting and participating in the political process. The poll tax was one of the ways that they kept black folks from voting, but this also prevented poor white people, of which there were many, from voting. Certainly, if you were poor and money was scarce, why would you pay money to vote?

Then there was the literacy test—another barrier put in place to prevent blacks from voting. This was a test that had to be passed before one could vote. It was extremely discriminatory, as part of the test was having potential voters read and interpret the Constitution. African Americans may have had to read and interpret 50 or more words, where whites only had to read and interpret eight. And then who graded the test? You guessed it: white folks who had a vested interest in the outcome of the election. Jim Crow was alive and kicking, for sure.

If a black man decided to vote, pay the tax, passed the test, and went to the polling station, there would be white people there harassing them—so it was just easier not to vote. They put obstacle after obstacle up to prevent black folks from voting, so why go? Again, I don't know anyone who voted back in the 1930s, '40s, or '50s. I am sure there were rebels who voted, but I did not know any of them.

I attended an all-black school, but the white people controlled what we learned, and maybe that is why I do not remember discussions about politics when I attended school. Although I was a lifelong reader of the newspaper, I just never thought about or focused on politics until later in life.

The first time I voted, I had been in the military for a number of years. It was probably in the 1960s, while we were stationed in Germany. This was probably 10 to 15 years after I joined the military. I am sure I voted for Kennedy and believe that I had to mail my vote back to the States. As I think back, I cannot tell you why I voted in that election, but I have voted in every presidential election since Kennedy and have always voted for the Democratic candidate. Absolutely I voted for President Obama and am elated that he won.

Voting is important to me today, so I still vote, although frequently I don't like any of the candidates running for a particular office. Today, I think it is extremely important for citizens to participate in our democracy. I would encourage everyone to vote and probably developed this philosophy about participating in the process gradually over time. Maybe age might have something to do with it, also.

Although I was not very politically engaged until the 1960s, I do remember *Brown v. Board of Education* in the 1950s. I was aware of this case, and I guess everyone else was aware of it at the time. It was in the headlines of every newspaper, and I have always read newspapers and continue to this day, into my 90s. I believe in freedom of choice but did not advocate for one side or the other in the Brown case.

I have always been a Democrat and have never voted Republican or Independent because when I started voting, blacks were Democrats. They seemed to be the most race conscious and seem to be on the side of the ordinary person—white or black. I associated Republicans with the right-wingers—people like George Wallace, Rush Limbaugh, Sarah Palin, and the FOX crowd. They really put a bad taste in my mouth. I do not know all of them because I am not inclined to watch or read about them due to their extremely negative views. I am sure that there are Democrats that are far left leaning also, but as a black person, I never focused on the left leaning Democrats.

However, to tell the truth, I do not care too much for Jessie Jackson, as his opinions are not balanced, and he simply cannot see the middle ground. He seems to be advocating race relations and the uplifting of blacks, but it seems as if he is doing it for personal glory—more like a politician, as opposed to someone who really cares about the condition of black people. This is so even though he marched with Dr. Martin Luther King, Jr. Jessie does not seem to be as genuine as some of the others who marched with Dr. King.

During his early years, when he was stumping with Dr. King, he seemed to be picture hungry, or glory hunting. Jessie seemed to want to be seen and heard. However, I absolutely did not have a problem with Dr. King. I think that most black people liked him, although I realize that he was not perfect either. I think that the difference between Jessie and other lieutenants of Dr. King, like Andrew Jackson and Elijah Cummings, was the attitude. Of course, two people can say the same thing, but if they have different attitudes, you come away liking one better than the other.

I disagree with conservatives who talk about poverty and handing things out to people for not doing anything. I believe that most people who have something to give, give. On the other hand, many people have a lot of money and choose not to give, even though they got their money by taking advantage of people who have less. I have no problem with welfare as a whole, but I certainly understand that there needs to be some tweaking of the system. I can even understand why others might have a problem with some parts of it. However, as far as the people who need assistance, I have absolutely no problem with them getting the support that they need.

I think that Republicans use religion and social issues to attract people to their cause, but I do not think that they can be successful with this strategy in the long run because of their overall extreme views, especially as it relates to race and poverty. The white church can focus on abortion and gay marriage, but the African American church has to focus their energy on their congregation's day-to-day activity of living. As for me, there is absolutely nothing in the Republican platform that is attractive; Republicans simply do not represent my interests. I do not believe that there is anything that they could come up with to attract me because I know that it would just be a smokescreen. In my opinion, there is little in the Republican platform that is attractive to blacks.

I believe that Republicans want to reduce social programs for black people, and the way to do that is to reduce taxes. But this hurts poor whites also, and the poor whites just don't see it that way. I believe that when poor white people vote Republican, it is absolutely a racial issue, and the most essential component that separates the two parties is race. On the other hand, I am a Democrat and also see Democrats though historically racial-tinted lenses. Through my lenses, the best presidents and my favorites were Barak Obama, John

Kennedy, Franklin Roosevelt, and to a lesser degree, Linden Johnson, although he did a lot for African Americans. Obama is my all-time favorite because he was compassionate and the most sympathetic to us. My least favorite is Trump. I like nothing, absolutely nothing about him.

I have no problem with people migrating to the United Sates legally, but I also have no problem with the government putting minefields along the border to keep the illegals out. Maybe this is Trumpism. I do not think that most illegal immigrants are evil or bad people, but they are illegal. Trying to escape from poverty may not be a bad thing, but it violates the law. Every nation in the world has rules and regulations about their borders, so we are no different, and we have to have laws.

I have no problem with the Affordable Care Act—"Obamacare." I am getting health care, which is socialized. My wife received socialized health care. We have gotten it since I retired almost 30 years ago. I imagine there are hundreds of thousands or millions of veterans receiving socialized medicine, and no one complains because it is not a bad thing. Why should anyone be against anyone for receiving health care? As much money as the rich people have, it is simply amazing to me that they are the ones who complain about helping people—especially with something as basic to living as health care. I guess since I am not in the group that has the most money, I can be for ensuring that people who do not have health care get it.

I do believe that there should be some checks and balances on almost everything. The average citizen cannot monitor or check big business, the banking industry, our food, or medical supplies, so there is a need for the government to be about the people's business. Politicians should make the rules because that is why we elect them; although I personally do not expect them to make legitimate rules because most are dishonest to their core. We, the citizens, should pressure politicians to do the right thing because they are responsible to the people. Societies should and must have agencies that prevent abuse. It is the people who must put pressure on politicians because there are not too many politicians who are concerned about social policy and the moral right. If they didn't have to keep up their image, they wouldn't be invested in it at all.

There are certain issues that the people feel strongly about; therefore, these issues get the politicians' attention. Welfare is a good example. Were politicians sincere about poor people they would have them at the forefront of their thinking and behavior. But to the contrary, most politicians do not really want to address welfare, regardless of party. Although some adults have legitimate welfare needs, it should mostly be about the children who must be fed and provided assistance. This includes clothing, medical care, and education.

Society and the Need for Change

People should do things legally, and they should follow the law, but there is a higher calling. We all also have a moral code, which we should follow. We the people should not do what we want to do because we can get away with it, or we probably would not stop at the small stuff. Even so, there are more evil people making laws than good people. To me, this means that the evil people are making rules that negatively impact good people. This is where civil disobedience and violence is justified and required, and it is why people such as Gandhi and King were so valued.

Take slavery, for instance. I believe that a majority of the people, even most whites, didn't believe that slavery was right, but it lasted for hundreds of years. And so, uprisings like John Brown and Harpers Ferry were justified; more people should have rebelled because slavery was just wrong.

White people used the justification that the American Negro was no better than an animal. They say that when the slave traders went to Africa, they found animals that looked like humans. They had paint on the faces and body and piercings and such. These animals were dancing and moving in such a manner that they could not be human. Yet, in America, these beings were domesticated and learned to talk, laugh, read, learn trades. They had super common sense, but they were still held in bondage as if they were animals.

The indignity that was perpetrated on the Native Americans were even worse than that of slaves. Certainly, there was a conscious attempt to eradicate the Native American. There is no justification for this thinking or behavior. I am certain, however, that to this day there are some who don't view blacks as equal in our society.

One has to know when a law is legal and legitimate and/or illegal and illegitimate, and therefore when it is right to violate that law. When one breaks a law for personal gain, it is different from when one is trying to change a law for the common good of the masses. Even so, if people do things for themselves and it benefits the group, then that might not be a bad thing.

Malcolm X was trying to change some of the big things that were wrong in our society, such as racism, and I admired him for it. I supported everything he did, to include his radical tactics. I also supported Elijah Muhammad's philosophy and methods, although he may not have been the most moral individual—not unlike many Christian clergy today.

Malcolm X had a philosophy that said by any means necessary, and I support this practice. I agree with Dr. King's philosophy, up to a point. You should not start violence, but if you are trying to right a wrong, I do not have a problem with one supporting and defending themselves with violence. I would not favor Malcolm as an individual over Dr. King, but I do not have a problem with his approach. I absolutely believe that if you get punched, you should punch back, hard!

The Black Panthers were too radical for me, and I do not believe that their means justified what they were trying to accomplish. I believe that they just wanted to incite violence, and therefore they were no better than the people they were against, but I could very well be wrong.

I do believe that African Americans can be empowered through education, and although I only obtained a high school education, it was my vision that my children would obtain higher levels of education. To this end, it was my responsibility to finance their undergraduate educations, which I did. Additionally, I believe that I helped plant the seed in all of my children that education is invaluable, and to this end, all of my children have at least a bachelor's degree. As noted before, three have obtained terminal or doctorate degrees.

I strongly disagree with W. E. B. Du Bois' theory about "the talented tenth," where only a tenth of African Americans possess what is required to succeed in higher education and society. Further, I do not believe that there are insufficient numbers of professional jobs to sustain employment for more than a tenth of the African American population, the college graduates, as proposed by W. E. B. Du Bois. I believe that if you can go to college, it is beneficial regardless of the employment opportunities. It is personally beneficial and beneficial to society for its members to be educated, regardless of whether it is in the physical or social sciences or liberal arts.

I rest my case. I/we have come a long way over the past century. Even so, we—or I should say *you*—must continue to push on. It is my belief that through strong family values, true religious or spiritual convictions, education, and hard work, we can have a more balanced and stress free life. I stand convinced that the world should be our playground.

Thank you for taking the time to read my story.

About the Author

Douglas Newsome is the third of Henian and Essie Nora's four children. He penned his father's story after spending countless summer days sitting on the porch and winter evenings sitting in the comfort of their house listening to his reflections on his life. The author has advanced degrees in psychology and education, and he is the sole owner of Zen Philosophy Consultants, LLC.

Consistent with the Zen tradition, he has dedicated his life to helping others live healthier, more peaceful, and satisfying lives, where generosity is paramount. This is the author's first book, and it is hoped that a peek into the life of his father, who is about to become a centenarian, can give his descendants and people far and wide insight, knowledge, and wisdom into playing the hand life gives them; to overcoming suffering; and to live a joyous, productive life.

Comments from the author's daughter, Dana:

> So, my dad wrote a book (KUDOS TO HIM) about his father. He's asked me to read over it and let him know my opinion. Man, I've learned sooooo

much about my grandfather and family that I never knew. I'm soooo proud of the person he is, and I'm proud to be a Newsome.

My granddad told me he could have passed for white growing up (some of his buddies did), but he was proud to be a black man. I never really thought too much into it, but in the book, my granddad was in the military, in a black line, preparing for training. A white officer told him to go get in the correct line. My granddad told that officer that he was in the right line—the black line. WOW!

www.ingramcontent.com/pod-product-compliance
Lightning Source LLC
Chambersburg PA
CBHW051943290426
44110CB00015B/2095